A Guide to SPSS
for Analysis of Variance

A Guide to SPSS
for Analysis of Variance

Gustav Levine

Arizona State University

 LAWRENCE ERLBAUM ASSOCIATES, PUBLISHERS

1991   Hillsdale, New Jersey   Hove and London

Lawrence Erlbaum Associates, Inc., Publishers
365 Broadway
Hillsdale, New Jersey 07642

Library of Congress Cataloging-in-Publication Data

Levine, Gustav.
    A guide to SPSS for analysis of variance / Gustav Levine.
    p.   cm.
    Includes bibliographical references and index.
    ISBN 0-8058-0939-2. -- ISBN 0-8058-0941-4 (pbk.)
    1. SPSS (Computer program) 2. Analysis of variance--Computer
programs. I. Title.
    HA31.35.L48   1991
    519.5'0285'5329--dc20   90-21162
                                                        CIP

Printed in the United States of America

10 9 8 7 6 5 4 3

To Sandy Braver
who enjoys being helpful

Table of Contents

Preface

This manual provides detailed examples of programs for analysis of variance and related statistical tests of significance that can be run with releases 3 and 4 of the SPSS statistical software package. The purpose is to provide complete sets of commands that can be directly copied, with only names or numbers of levels of factors having to be changed. Ways to alter command specifications to fit situations with larger numbers of factors are discussed and illustrated, along with ways to combine program statements to request a variety of analyses in the same program.

It is assumed that the manual will often be used when a single design is of momentary interest. All of the chapters have the types of designs as major headings, so a specific design can be readily located (e.g., completely randomized, repeated measures, or mixed). Each chapter focuses on a particular type of test (for example simple effects, multiple comparisons, trend analyses), further simplifying identification of the needed sets of commands. In addition, each of the chapters has its own concluding section on reading the printouts for the type of information discussed in that chapter.

Chapters 1 and 2 are the basic chapters to be read by people not already familiar with SPSS. Chapter 1 gives detailed programs for obtaining omnibus F tests in completely randomized designs. Chapter 2 gives the same type of information for designs that include repeated measures factors. General rules concerning the use of specific commands, subcommands, and keywords, are also discussed in these two chapters, offering a highly specfic introduction to the use of SPSS for analysis of variance.

Having read Chapters 1 and 2 it is then possible to read the other chapters independently, in any order. People who have become familiar with SPSS through running a couple of programs may find that they can skim Chapters 1 and 2. Chapters 3 through 7 have been written with just enough redundancy so that it is not necessary to go through the complete manual when dealing with a single design or a single type of test.

GETTING ON THE COMPUTER

SPSS is available at most colleges and universities on mainframe computers, and there is a PC version that is now available. Some knowledge of the particular computer system, and how SPSS is to be accessed is necessary, for mainframe users. This usually requires only two or three commands in some job control language (JCL), along with a couple of JCL closing statements for telling the computer to run the program. For example, on an IBM 3090 OS/MVS system, using WYLBUR, you can generally access SPSS by typing three commands, COLLECT, // JOB, and // EXEC SPSSX. These are job control language statements that can differ from one mainframe situation to another. Once the few JCL statements needed for a particular mainframe system are learned, they can be used with all SPSS programs. This manual assumes that the user will obtain these JCL statements at the site where the program is to be run.

Gustav Levine

List of Programs

MULTIPLE COMPARISONS, ONE FACTOR, COMPLETELY RANDOMIZED

CONTRASTS WITH MULTIPLE FACTORS

Completely Randomized

Contrasts on Repeated Measures

Mixed Designs

Simple Effects of Contrasts

1 Basic Commands and Omnibus F Tests for Completely Randomized Designs

This chapter has a dual role: to explain the use of relevant program commands, and to offer sets of program statements for omnibus F tests in completely randomized designs. Therefore this chapter includes general discussion of how to use SPSS, along with the illustrations of the statements needed for specific completely randomized designs. The assumption is made that SPSS has been accessed from the main frame, so only the statements within the SPSS program are displayed in the examples.

BASIC ANALYSIS OF VARIANCE COMMANDS

The basic analysis of variance commands will be presented in capital letters. It wil be useful to begin by displaying a set of hypothetical data from three groups of subjects, following that with a sample program for analyzing the data with the analysis of variance statistic. The data appear in Fig. 1.1.

In the example presented in Fig. 1.1, different subjects are assumed in each of the three groups, with just one factor in the design, and observations on one variable. A design with one factor and different subjects in the different groups is usually identified as a completely randomized one factor analysis of variance, which the SPSS program calls up with the command ONEWAY.

The program, presented below in Fig. 1.2, is followed with an explanation of the function of the different commands in the program, and the variations in the commands that might be found useful. The commands that are to be typed into the computer will all be presented below in capital

Group 1	Group 2	Group 3
1	3	4
2	4	4
4	5	6
2	5	3
2	3	3

FIG. 1.1. Hypothetical data for a one factor completely randomized design, with five subjects in each group.

letters (although they do not have to be typed as upper case). It is assumed that a key press will follow each command (each program statement), to enter each command, using either a specific ⟨ENTER⟩ key, or a ⟨RETURN⟩ key (the key used differing with different computer facilities and keyboards). These ⟨ENTER⟩ presses are omitted in Fig. 1.2 and subsequent illustrations of programs. The numbers in the figures that precede each of the program statements are there only for easy reference within this text.

The first statement in Fig. 1.2, TITLE, is an optional command that is used for easy identification of different programs you might be running. The command TITLE tells the computer that what follows on that line is the title that you will want to see in the printout. What you write on that line is only for your information, and does not affect the analysis. It is necessary that a space separates the command TITLE from the actual title. In the printout you will then see that line appearing, minus the word TITLE, on the top of the pages of the printout. If you wish to use a long

```
 1. TITLE CR ONE FACTOR A/V
 2. DATA LIST LIST/GROUP SCORE
 3. ONEWAY SCORE BY GROUP (1,3)
 4.   /STATISTICS = DESCRIPTIVES
 5. BEGIN DATA
 6. 1 1
 7. 1 2
 8. 1 4
 9. 1 2
10. 1 2
11. 2 3
12. 2 4
13. 2 5
14. 2 5
15. 2 3
16. 3 4
17. 3 4
18. 3 6
19. 3 3
20. 3 3
21. END DATA
```

FIG. 1.2. Program for a completely randomized one factor analysis of variance.

descriptive title that will identify the program for you in some detailed fashion, you may have to continue the title on the next line. To do this, simply indent the second line one space. However, SPSS will only repeat the first sixty letters of the title at the top of every page; the full title only appearing where the program itself is reproduced. The way to add additional descriptive information to the top of every page is to use the SUBTITLE command. This command is entered in the same way as the TITLE command. It is placed on the line following the TITLE command, with the actual subtitle separated from the SUBTITLE command by a space. For example,

```
SUBTITLE EXAMPLE FROM THE MANUAL
```

will produce, as a second line of description at the top of every page of the printout, the words EXAMPLE FROM THE MANUAL.

Look at the second program statement. The first part of the line,

```
DATA LIST
```

is always used in an SPSS analysis of variance program. The rest of the line involves options that can change from one version of the program to another. The specifications in the DATA LIST statement are discussed further in the following paragraphs. The specifications can be sufficiently extensive to require a second line. If this is the case, you simply indent at least one space on the continuing line. For example, statement 2 from Fig. 1.2 can be typed in either of the two following ways:

```
2. DATA LIST LIST
     /GROUP SCORE
```

or

```
2. DATA LIST LIST/GROUP
     SCORE
```

Using Stored Data

If the data are already stored in the computer, and do not have to be entered with the program, you have to identify your data file so that it can be retrieved. This is done with the FILE subcommand of the DATA LIST command. For example, if your data file was named URGENT, your DATA LIST program statement would look like the following:

```
DATA LIST FILE=URGENT LIST/GROUP SCORE
```

However, the particular computer and its operating system will probably require additional specifications for locating and retrieving the program from within the system. Such information can only be obtained at the local computer site. It would consist of some additional specifications within the DATA LIST program statement. This is the only line within the set of SPSS program statements that will vary with the computer facilities. Variations in that one statement are less likely to be needed when the data is included with the SPSS program statements. Consequently, in this manual, it is assumed that the data is entered with the SPSS commands and subcommands. When this is the case, the DATA LIST specifications given here should suffice. In many instances in this manual illustrative data are given with the programs, in order to illustrate the data input. In the current version of SPSS it is assumed that the data are inline (present, in the same file with the other SPSS commands), unless otherwise specified in the DATA LIST statement.

Options for Listing Data

There are three options available for presenting data in SPSS, each associated with a keyword. The three keywords are LIST, FIXED, and FREE. FIXED is the default, so when it is used it does not have to be specified.

Proper Form for Listing Data in the LIST Format.   The program is informed of the manner of data presentation by the use of a keyword just preceding the slash in the DATA LIST command. For example,

```
DATA LIST LIST/GROUP SCORE
```

contains the word LIST in that position. The LIST data format has two implications. One, is that the information on each subject will appear in a separate entry (on a separate line or set of lines). Second, the information will appear within the entry in the order indicated after the slash, as in

```
. . . . . /GROUP SCORE,
```

which tells the computer that the first number in each entry is called GROUP and the second number is called SCORE. This arrangement is followed for the data in Fig. 1.2.

Any single word with eight or less letters (and numbers) can be used to identify a component of the data, as long as the name begins with a letter. The first word following the slash is usually (although not necessarily) the name of the factor. It could usefully be given a name such as DOSAGE, rather than GROUP, if drug dosage was the factor being tested. The second name, SCORE, could usefully be replaced by YEARS, if that was what was being observed or measured. In other words, the factor and the set of observations are given names in the DATA LIST statement, and the order of the information for each subject is made clear.

Look back at Fig. 1.2, beginning with line 6, and observe the succeeding rows. The first number in each row ranges between one and three; that is because there are three levels in the factor, so the numbers 1, 2, or 3 are used to indicate a specific level of the factor. The first five subjects (each having a separate line) are in the first group, the next five in the second, etc. The second number for each subject refers to that subject's score. It is in this sense that the data for each subject are mirrored in the order of names following the slash in the DATA LIST command (. . . /GROUP SCORE).

The next program statement in Fig. 1.2 is

```
ONEWAY SCORE BY GROUP(1,3)
```

that calls up the one factor completely randomized analysis of variance package within SPSS (through the word ONEWAY). The part of the sentence after ONEWAY always specifies the observation first (in this case SCORE), so that the program will know, from the position of the word SCORE, what it refers to; and will know that the factor is called GROUP, by its position (since it comes second, right after the word BY in the ONEWAY command statement). That is, the name for the variable being observed (the scores) always follows the word ONEWAY and *precedes* the word BY, while the name for the factor always *follows* the word BY. The name designating the factor is immediately followed by a pair of parentheses that contains the information on the levels of the factor. That is, the levels have to be numbered, and the parentheses contain the range of these numbers. For example, if there are two groups, use (1,2); if three groups (1,3); if four, (1,4); etc. The second number in the parentheses in essence indicates the number of levels of the factor. Thus, the program statement

```
ONEWAY SCORE BY GROUP(1,3)
```

indicates that the one factor completely randomized analysis of variance is to be done on a set of scores from three different groups, identified as levels one through three of a factor called GROUP, where the variable being measured or observed is called SCORE. The computer can then look back at line 2 (program statement 2).

```
DATA LIST LIST/GROUP SCORE
```

and know that the first number on each line will designate which group a score comes from, and the second number is an actual score (because of the order of the names GROUP and SCORE following the DATA LIST command). Further, because of the numbers in parentheses in line 3 (1,3) the computer knows that it has to compute the analysis with three groups, coded 1, 2, 3. The computer will be able to identify the group from which a score has come by the first number it encounters, and the observation by the second number it encounters. To distinguish the numbers, they should be separated by at least one space when using the LIST format for data entry.

The only critical requirement for names is that the program be consistent in the use of the names in the DATA LIST and ONEWAY commands, and that the names be made up of no more than eight letters or numbers, although never beginning with a number. However, there are some sets of letters that can form keywords for some commands, and so should be avoided as names. The sets of letters that you should not use as names are the following: ALL, AND, BY, EQ, GE, GT, LE, LT, NE, NOT, OR, TO, and WITH.

Identifying Individual Subjects.   Sometimes it is desirable to number individual subjects. When this is the case an additional number is required in each entry. The program statement could then look like

```
DATA LIST LIST/ID GROUP SCORE
```

and the data itself would be entered in the form

```
1 1 22
2 1 19
3 1 9
4 1 25
etc.
```

where the first number in each entry represents a subject's ID, the second the factor level, and the third number is the actual score.

```
9 2 5
10 2 3
11 3 4
etc.
```

Proper Form for Listing Data in the FIXED Format.   An alternative to the LIST data format is called the FIXED data format. It consists of always having the data in specific specified columns. The program can be prepared for this arrangement of the data by the use of the word FIXED in place of the second use of the word LIST, or else by simply omitting any format designation, since FIXED is the default. For example, using the data as presented in Fig. 1.2, the factor level for each subject is in the first column, the second column is simply a space, with the score of each subject in the third column. If the FIXED format were used to present the same data, this column specificity would be added to the DATA LIST command as follows:

```
DATA LIST FIXED/GROUP 1 SCORE 3.
```

or since, FIXED is the default,

```
DATA LIST/GROUP 1 SCORE 3.
```

The number after GROUP indicates the column indexing the factor level, and the number after SCORE indicates the column giving the score of each subject. If the scores required more than one column (say some of the scores were two digit values) the values following SCORE would be 3–4:

```
DATA LIST/GROUP 1 SCORE 3-4.
```

That is, the range of columns are shown with an intervening hyphen when more than one column is used. Assume some two digit values in the data. The data as entered into the program would then take the following form:

```
1  8
1  6
1 11
2  7
2 12
etc.
```

If the researcher desires to include numbers for the individual subjects, an additional pair of columns would be required (assuming numbers of subjects between 1 and 99). The program statement might then look like

```
DATA LIST/ID 1-2 GROUP 4 SCORE 6-7.
```

and the data would be entered in the form

```
1 1  8
2 1  6
3 1 11
4 2  7
5 2 12
etc.
```

In summary, for the FIXED data format the column numbers are specified in the DATA LIST command; and the identifying information and data then have to appear at the specified locations.

Presenting Data Horizontally in the FREE Format. There is a third format for entering and processing the data, which is signaled by the use of the word FREE in place of either LIST or FIXED. The FREE format involves presenting all of the scores and their coded group membership consecutively, with a space between each number. This, like the LIST method, requires that the order of the information be specified following the slash in the DATA LIST command. But the use of the word FREE in the statement will indicate to the computer that the order will be continuously repeated, and not necessarily placed on separate lines. Thus the information for a number of subjects could all appear on the same line, if there is sufficient room. For example, the following statement

```
DATA LIST FREE/GROUP SCORE
```

would mean the first, third, fifth, etc. numbers encountered on the line following BEGIN DATA.would indicate group membership, and the second, fourth, sixth, etc. numbers would indicate the actual scores of people from the respective groups indicated by the first, third, and fifth numbers. The program presented in Fig. 1.2 would then look like

```
1. TITLE CR ONE FACTOR A/V
2. DATA LIST FREE/GROUP SCORE
3. ONEWAY SCORE BY GROUP(1,3)
4.    /STATISTICS=DESCRIPTIVES
5. BEGIN DATA
6. 1 1 1 2 1 4 1 2 1 2 2 3 2 4 2 5 2 5 2 3 3 4 3 4 3 6 3 3 3 3
7. END DATA
```

If it was necessary to include subject ID's, the second program statement would be presented as

```
DATA LIST FREE/ID GROUP SCORE
```

and the data would be entered as ordered triples:

```
1 1 1 2 1 2 3 1 4 4 1 2 5 1 2 etc.
```

The listing in this horizontal fashion can continue on as many lines as needed, until all the data are entered.

Requesting the Analysis of Variance

Statement 3 in the program seen in Fig. 1.2 is:

```
ONEWAY SCORE BY GROUP(1,3).
```

This indicates the inferential statistic that is to be computed (completely randomized one factor analysis of variance). For a completely randomized design with more than one factor the word ANOVA would replace ONE-WAY.

Specifying Multiple Factors

As indicated earlier, the words SCORE BY GROUP(1,3), in program statement 3 in Fig. 1.2, indicate the observed or measured variable (SCORE) and the factor (GROUP). The different levels in the factor are identifed with the numbers in parentheses where, for example, (1,3) signifies three levels to be coded 1, 2, and 3.

If doing a completely randomized *two* factor analysis of variance, the two identifying labels for the two factors would follow the word BY, each separated by a space, and each indicating its own levels. Also, in place of the ONEWAY command, you would use the ANOVA command. Specifically,

```
ANOVA SCORE BY A(1,2) B(1,4)
```

would signify a completely randomized two factor analysis with two factors, A and B.

It will sometimes be advantageous to use words rather than single letters to name factors. However, be careful not to use spaces as a part of the factor name. For example, assume that the two factors are called FAC-TORA and FACTORB. The program statement would then be

```
ANOVA SCORE BY FACTORA(1,2) FACTORB(1,4).
```

The computer uses spaces to separate factors on that line, so if you separated the A from the rest of the factor name, as in FACTOR A, the computer would be receiving information that there are three factors present, a factor called FACTOR, another called A, and a third called FAC-TORB.

Entering Data with Multiple Factors

In a two factor design each score is nested in a particular combination of two levels of the two factors. That is, scores are each obtained under specific conditions involving both of the factors. In the data presentation, an additional number would be needed to indicate levels on the second factor.

For example, some scores would be obtained under the first level of the first factor, as well as under the first level of the second factor, while some other scores would be obtained under the second level of the first factor, but the fourth level of the second factor, etc. Thus each score would need two code numbers, one for each factor (to identify the levels of the two factors under which the score was obtained). This would require that two numbers be associated with each score, or three numbers for each entry in a LIST data format. For example, the first two data entries in the SPSS program, following the BEGIN DATA statement, might be

```
1 1 3
1 1 2
    .
    .
    .
```

suggesting that two of the scores in the cell at the first level of both variables, are 3 and 2. A later entry, if

```
    .
    .
2 3 5
    .
    .
    .
```

would mean that there is a score of 5, in the cell at the second level of the first factor, and the third level of the second factor. In Fig. 1.3, which gives an example of an SPSS program for a completely randomized two factor analysis of variance, both factors have just two levels. Again the example uses inline data (data included within the program).

In the DATA LIST command indicating which columns represent which events, you would give the names of the two factors first, since they would be indicated within the first and second columns, and then the name for the observed variable (here SCORE). With the three different DATA formats, (LIST, FREE, and FIXED) you would have the option of three different specifications in the DATA LIST command:

```
DATA LIST LIST/FACTORA FACTORB SCORE
DATA LIST FREE/FACTORA FACTORB SCORE
DATA LIST/FACTORA 1 FACTORB 3 SCORE 5
```

unless you required two columns for some scores, in which case, for the FIXED method, you would have

```
DATA LIST/FACTORA 1 FACTORB 3 SCORE 5-6.
```

Adding More Factors to the Design.   If you had three factors, designated A, B, and C, each with three levels, the DATA LIST and ANOVA program statements could look like the following:

```
DATA LIST LIST/A B C SCORE
ANOVA SCORE BY A(1,3) B(1,3) C(1,3).
```

```
 1.  TITLE CR TWO FACTOR A/V
 2.  DATA LIST LIST/FACTORA FACTORB SCORE
 3.  ANOVA SCORE BY FACTORA(1,2) FACTORB(1,2)
 4.     /STATISTICS = MEAN
 5.  BEGIN DATA
 6.  1 1 3
 7.  1 1 2
 8.  1 1 3
 9.  1 1 4
10.  1 1 3
11.  1 1 3
12.  1 2 5
13.  1 2 6
14.  1 2 7
15.  1 2 8
16.  1 2 5
17.  1 2 4
18.  2 1 1
19.  2 1 2
20.  2 1 3
21.  2 1 1
22.  2 1 3
23.  2 1 2
24.  2 2 7
25.  2 2 8
26.  2 2 8
27.  2 2 7
28.  2 2 9
29.  2 2 9
30.  END DATA
```

FIG. 1.3. Program for a completely randomized two factor analysis of variance analyzed with SPSS.

For four factors, with A and B having three levels, but factors C and D having four levels, the program statements could be:

```
DATA LIST LIST/A B C D SCORE
ANOVA SCORE BY A(1,3) B(1,3) C(1,4) D(1,4)
```

etc.

For the data set, each additional factor would require that an additional number be included, to designate the level of that factor for each score. In a completely randomized design with four factors, there would be five numbers in each entry (each row of the data), but only the last number in each row would represent an actual score, the first four being devoted to identifying the levels of the factors.

The Statistics Subcommand (Descriptive Statistics)

The only remaining program statement that offers an option is statement number four in Figs. 1.2 and 1.3:

```
STATISTICS = DESCRIPTIVES
```

in Fig. 1.2; and

```
STATISTICS=MEAN
```

in Fig. 1.3.

With the ONEWAY command, the STATISTICS subcommand uses the keyword DESCRIPTIVE to get the usual descriptive statistics that are desired. It yields, for each group, the number of cases (n), the mean, the standard deviation, the standard error, the minimum, the maximum, and the 95% confidence interval. Tests for homogeneity of variance can be obtained with the key word HOMOGENEITY in place of DESCRIP-TIVES. To get both, use the keyword ALL, as in

```
/STATISTICS=ALL
```

With the ANOVA command, the STATISTICS subcommand has a different set of optional keywords. The most likely to be needed, is MEAN, which offers means of all the cells and marginals (levels of the factors), and the number of scores in each cell or level.

```
TITLE THREE FACTOR A/V, VARIABLE C COLLAPSED
DATA LIST LIST/A B C SCORE
ANOVA SCORE BY A(1,2) B(1,2)
   /STATISTICS=MEAN
BEGIN DATA
1 1 1 15
1 1 1 12
   . .
   . .

   . .
2 2 1 10
2 2 1 10
   . .
   . .

   . .
1 1 2 17
1 1 2 19
   . .

   . .
2 2 2 28
2 2 2 25
END DATA
```

FIG. 1.4.   Three factor completely randomized design with three factors, one of them collapsed in the analysis. That is, the distinctions (levels) of factor C are ignored in the analysis, simply by not mentioning that factor in the specifications for the ANOVA command. (As usual, the verbalization in the title does not affect the program.)

COLLAPSING (IGNORING) A FACTOR

Assume a three factor completely randomized design, where one of the factors is gender. You did the analysis, and found that gender was not statistically significant, and that the gender related differences were so small that it was clearly not an appropriate variable for this analysis. You might now wish to look at the analysis with gender removed as a variable, and ignore gender in any further analyses. Doing this is quite simple in a completely randomized design. In the program statement containing the ANOVA command, simply omit any reference to the factor you wish to ignore. Fig. 1.4 gives an example of a three factor completely randomized design in which factor C is not mentioned in the ANOVA command specifications, and so is ignored in the analysis. (The analysis uses all of the data, but does not separate scores in terms of the levels of factor C).

READING THE PRINTOUTS FOR COMPLETELY RANDOMIZED DESIGNS

The SPSS statements that you have entered appear early in the printout, minus JCL (job control language) statements, and usually minus data and the BEGIN DATA and END DATA commands. The program is followed by some descriptive information (means, standard deviations, etc.), and by significance tests. What appears in the printout varies both with the commands given, and with the designs.

Omnibus *F* Tests in CR One Factor Designs

A one factor completely randomized design (a single between subjects factor) is generally run under the ONEWAY command, where the descriptive information, if requested, uncharacteristically *follows* the analysis of variance summary table.

Descriptive Information. If the STATISTICS = DESCRIPTIVES subcommand and keyword are included, then the descriptive information consists of a listing of the means and standard deviations of the scores in the different groups, minimum and maximum values in each group, and confidence intervals for the means.

Analysis of Variance Summary Tables. The form of the analysis of variance table for the one factor completely randomized design is the usual one found in most textbooks. It includes the sources of variance broken down into BETWEEN GROUPS, WITHIN GROUPS, and TOTAL sums

ANALYSIS OF VARIANCE

SOURCE	D.F.	SUM OF SQUARES	MEAN SQUARES	F RATIO	F PROB.
BETWEEN GROUPS	2	10.8000	5.4000	4.3784	.0373
WITHIN GROUPS	12	14.8000	1.2333		
TOTAL	14	25.6000			

FIG. 1.5.   Analysis of variance table for the one factor completely randomized design presented in Figure 1.2 of this chapter, as it would appear in an SPSS printout.

of squares, the degrees of freedom and mean squares for each, and the F ratio along with the probability value for F. The example of a program for a one factor completely randomized design given in Fig. 1.2 in this chapter, would yield a table like that seen in Fig. 1.5.

If the program did not run, you would find error statements on the last page of the printout.

Omnibus *F* Tests in CR Multifactor Designs

For multifactor completely randomized designs (multiple between subjects factors), the descriptive information, if requested, appears before the analysis of variance summary tables.

Descriptive Information.   With the STATISTICS = MEAN subcommand and keyword included, the first thing following the program is the grand mean (under the title TOTAL POPULATION); then, with the levels of the factors labeled 1, 2, etc., a listing of row and column means; and finally the cell means presented in the form of a matrix. Numbers of subjects contributing to each mean appear below their respective means. An example is given in Fig. 1.6, which is taken from the program and data for a two factor completely randomized design presented in Fig. 1.3 of this chapter, where the factors are labeled FACTORA and FACTORB, and each has two levels.

Analysis of Variance Summary Tables.   The summary table for the completely randomized two factor analysis of variance as requested in Fig. 1.3 of this chapter, is presented in Fig. 1.7.

As seen in Fig. 1.7, the sums of squares, mean squares, and degrees of freedom are given for each factor, and for the interaction. FACTORA in the example is the label for one main effect, and FACTORB is the label for the other. The interaction is labeled with the two factors involved in the interaction, FACTORA FACTORB. The within group sum of squares

```
                              CELL MEANS
        SCORE
   BY FACTORA
      FACTORB

TOTAL POPULATION
      (4.71)
  (      24 )

FACTORA
      1              2

      4.42         5.00
  (     12) (       12)

FACTORB
      1              2

      2.50         6.92
  (     12) (       12)

              FACTORB
                 1       2
FACTORA
         1      3.00    5.83
             (   6) (    6)

         2      2.00    8.00
             (   6) (    6)
```

FIG. 1.6. Descriptive data in a two factor completely randomized design. The values are those that would appear in an SPSS program for the data given in Fig. 1.3 of this chapter. The bottom "matrix" has the levels of FACTORB on the top, and the levels of FACTORA at the left margin. The eight values in the matrix are the means of each cell and, in parentheses, the ns in each cell, just as the numbers below the TOTAL POPULATION are the overall mean, and, in parentheses, the overall n.

ANALYSIS OF VARIANCE

```
              SCORE
      BY      FACTORA
              FACTORB
```

SOURCE OF VARIATION	SUM OF SQUARES	DF	MEAN SQUARE	F	SIGNIF OF F
MAIN EFFECTS	119.083	2	59.542	57.160	0.000
FACTORA	2.042	1	2.042	1.960	0.177
FACTORB	117.042	1	117.042	112.360	0.000
2-WAY INTERACTIONS	15.042	1	15.042	14.440	0.001
FACTORA FACTORB	15.042	1	15.042	14.440	0.001
EXPLAINED	134.125	3	44.708	42.920	0.000
RESIDUAL	20.833	20	1.042		
TOTAL	154.958	23	6.737		

FIG. 1.7. Analysis of variance summary table as it appears in SPSS for a two factor completely randomized design, using the data taken from Fig. 1.3 in this chapter.

appears here under the label "RESIDUAL." Additional terms (MAIN EFFECTS, 2-WAY INTERACTIONS, EXPLAINED,) are simply sums of some of the other sums of squares. For example, MAIN EFFECTS is the sum of the sums of squares over all of the individual main effects. The sum of squares for 2-WAY INTERACTIONS is redundant here with FAC-TORA FACTORB, but would have separate meaning in a three factor design, where 2-WAY INTERACTIONS would be the label for the sum of the sum of squares over all three 2-way interactions that would be tested in a three factor design. The EXPLAINED sum of squares is the sum of all of the sums of squares for all of the effects in the analysis (other than RESIDUAL).

2 Basic Commands and Omnibus F Tests for Designs with Repeated Measures

When you operate with repeated measures you have to use the MANOVA command rather than the ANOVA or ONEWAY commands. The MANOVA command permits a far greater variety of analyses, which in turn requires the user to choose among options. This is done through selection of optional subcommands (and keywords that offer further specification of options). The examples that follow will provide the necessary subcommands and keywords, and indicate when and how they are added to the MANOVA command.

ONE FACTOR REPEATED MEASURES DESIGNS

Figure 2.1 presents a hypothetical set of data for a one factor repeated measures design with four subjects.

Note that the first column in Fig. 2.1 indicates subjects, and that there are three levels of the factor (three measurements of each subject), which have been identified as A1, A2, and A3. Assume, initially, that the subjects' ID's are not included with the data in the program. The program is shown in Fig. 2.2a.

The first line in the program in Fig. 2.2a is the optional TITLE command, followed by an appropriate title. The second line in the program,

```
DATA LIST LIST/A1 A2 A3
```

includes LIST to specify the form in which the data are presented (as discussed earlier in chapter One); and following the slash, has the levels of

Subj.	A1	A2	A3
1	2	4	8
2	3	5	7
3	5	3	7
4	2	7	9

FIG. 2.1.   A hypothetical set of data for a one factor repeated measures design with four subjects.

the repeated measures factor. The levels of the repeated measures factor are always present somewhere after the slash. If the IDs are included with the data, as the first column in the data, then ID would precede the levels of the repeated measure, as in

    DATA LIST LIST/ID A1 A2 A3

although ID does not appear anywhere else within the program.

The third program statement in Fig. 2.2a, the MANOVA command,

    MANOVA A1 A2 A3

merely signifies that the MANOVA program is to be run, and that there are three levels of the repeated measures factor (called A1, A2, and A3). In the MANOVA command, it is permissible to use the word "to" as in A1 to A3, or, if there were six levels, A1 to A6, rather than specifying each level. (This would also be true with longer names, like ALCOHOL1 to ALCOHOL6.)

After the MANOVA command, there are several MANOVA subcommands that are qualifiers offering special instructions for the MANOVA program. Each subcommand is idented four spaces, placing the first letter of each subcommand under the O in MANOVA. However, each subcommand must be preceded by a slash, the slash either appearing on the same line, which puts the slash at the third space, as seen in Fig. 2.2a; or else the slash is positioned as the last character on the preceding line, which is illustrated in Fig. 2.2b. In the remainder of this manual the slash is consistently placed on the same line as the subcommand, as illustrated in Fig. 2.2a.

The first subcommand in Figs. 2.2a and 2.2b,

    WSFACTORS = A(3)

is an abbreviation for within subjects factors, which is another name for repeated measures factors (in contrast to between subjects factors). In the WSFACTORS subcommand the name of the within subjects factor (here simply A) is stated, along with the number of levels of the factor, the latter given in parentheses (3). Whereas the number of levels of between subjects factors are implied with a comma separating a 1 and the number of levels

```
 1.  TITLE ONE FACTOR REPEATED MEASURES A/V
 2.  DATA LIST LIST/A1 A2 A3
 3.  MANOVA A1 A2 A3
 4.    /WSFACTORS = A(3)
 5.    /PRINT = CELLINFO(MEANS)
 6.    /DESIGN
 7.  BEGIN DATA
 8.  2 4 8
 9.  3 5 7
10.  5 3 7
11.  5 7 9
12.  END DATA
```

FIG. 2.2a. Program for a one factor repeated measures design analyzed with the SPSS MANOVA program, with the slash placed at the beginning of subcommand lines.

```
 1.  TITLE ONE FACTOR REPEATED MEASURES A/V
 2.  DATA LIST LIST/A1 A2 A3
 3.  MANOVA A1 A2 A3/
 4.    WSFACTORS = A(3)/
 5.    PRINT = CELLINFO(MEANS)/
 6.    DESIGN
 7.  BEGIN DATA
 8.  2 4 8
 9.  3 5 7
10.  5 3 7
11.  5 7 9
12.  END DATA
```

FIG. 2.2b. Program for a one factor repeated measures design analyzed with the SPSS-X MANOVA program, with the slash placed at the end of the preceding line.

[as in (1,2) for two levels, (1,3) for three levels, etc.]; with repeated measures factors the number of levels are stated more simply, just using the number enclosed in parentheses, as in (2), or (3), etc. The WSFACTORS subcommand can only be used once in a given MANOVA command, and must immediately follow the MANOVA command in the sequence of commands.

The next subcommand, program statement 5,

```
PRINT = CELLINFO(MEANS)
```

is used to control which material appears in the printout, through the part of the subcommand following the equals sign. The program in Figs. 2.2a and 2.2b uses

```
CELLINFO(MEANS)
```

to instruct the program to present the means and standard deviations of the individual cells.

The final subcommand, program statement 6,

```
DESIGN
```

is always necessary as the last subcommand.

The data are presented in columns that follow the sequence in which the levels of the factor were ordered in the DATA LIST statement (A1 A2 A3). Thus the columns are synonymous with the levels, so, in contrast to designs using between subjects factors, there is no need for additional columns indicating levels of the factors.

MULTIFACTOR REPEATED MEASURES DESIGNS

Programs for multiple repeated measures with no between subjects factors are all similar to the basic programs for a single repeated measure. The few small differences occur within the first few program statements. Fig. 2.3 presents some hypothetical data for three subjects in a two factor repeated measures design, and Fig. 2.4 offers a sample program for analyzing these data.

Each column of data in Fig. 2.3 can be symbolized in terms of its levels on both factors. This would yield, from left to right, four levels, symbolized within the program as A1B1 A1B2 A2B1 A2B2. Each subject receives four different measurements, one under each of these levels of the two factors. These symbols (A1B1 A1B2 A2B1 A2B2) are then used in the program statements wherever it is necessary to represent the different levels. With these symbols understood, the program for a two factor repeated measures design seen in Fig. 2.4 can be recognized as almost identical to the program for the one factor repeated measures design in Fig. 2.2a.

Subj.	A1		A2	
	B1	B2	B1	B2
1	1	3	2	6
2	2	5	4	8
3	4	5	5	7

FIG. 2.3.   Hypothetical data for a two factor repeated measures design.

```
 1. TITLE TWO FACTOR REPEATED MEASURES A/V
 2. DATA LIST LIST/A1B1 A1B2 A2B1 A2B2
 3. MANOVA A1B1 A1B2 A2B1 A2B2
 4.    /WSFACTORS = A(2) B(2)
 5.    /PRINT = CELLINFO(MEANS)
 6.    /DESIGN
 7. BEGIN DATA
 8. 1 3 2 6
 9. 2 5 4 8
10. 4 5 5 7
11. END DATA
```

FIG. 2.4.   Program for a two factor repeated measures design analyzed with the SPSS MANOVA program.

Note that program statements 2 and 3 match in that they both list the same levels in the same order. Program statement 4, the first subcommand,

```
WSFACTORS = A(2) B(2)
```

gives the names for the factors, along with the number of levels of each factor. The order of these factors is important. The factor that "changes more slowly" is always placed first (factor A in this example). The phrase "changes more slowly" refers to the levels of the factor as we move from left to right in Fig. 2.3, as summarized in the sequence A1B1 A1B2 A2B1 A2B2 found in lines two and three of Fig. 2.4. Note that the levels of B change in the first two components in the sequence from B1 to B2, while A remains as A1, not changing until the third component (in A2B1). Thus A "changes more slowly," in this listing of conditions, so that factor A appears first after the equals sign in the WSFACTORS command.

If a third repeated measure, factor C, were included, it should be clear as to how to extrapolate from Figs. 2.2a and 2.4 to a program for a three factor repeated measures design. Assuming two levels for factor C, as well as for the other two factors, the data could be organized as seen in Fig. 2.5, and the program statements would look like those seen in Fig. 2.6.

		A1				A2		
	B1		B2		B1		B2	
Subj.	C1	C2	C1	C2	C1	C2	C1	C2
1	5	7	3	10	7	11	5	9
2	4	9	5	8	4	8	5	8
.	.	.	.	.	.	.	.	.
.	.	.	.	.	.	.	.	.

FIG. 2.5. One way of tabling data for a three factor repeated measures design. A is changing most slowly, and C is changing most quickly, in this way of organizing the data.

```
TITLE THREE FACTOR REPEATED MEASURES A/V
DATA LIST LIST/A1B1C1 A1B1C2 A1B2C1 A1B2C2 A2B1C1
  A2B1C2 A2B2C1 A2B2C2
MANOVA A1B1C1 A1B1C2 A1B2C1 A1B2C2 A2B1C1 A2B1C2 A2B2C1
  A2B2C2
  /WSFACTORS = A(2) B(2) C(2)
  /PRINT = CELLINFO(MEANS)
  /DESIGN
BEGIN DATA

    .
    .

END DATA
```

FIG. 2.6. Program statements for a three factor repeated measures design, with the data organized and labeled as in Fig. 2.5, where A changes most slowly, and C most quickly.

```
TITLE THREE FACTOR REPEATED MEASURES A/V
DATA LIST LIST/A1B1C1 A1B1C2 A1B2C1 A1B2C2 A2B1C1
 A2B1C2 A2B2C1 A2B2C2
MANOVA A1B1C1 A1B1C2 A1B2C1 A1B2C2 A2B1C1 A2B1C2 A2B2C1
 A2B2C2
  /WSFACTORS = A(2)
    B(2) C(2)
  /PRINT = CELLLINFO(MEANS)
  /DESIGN
BEGIN DATA
 .
 .
 .
END DATA
```

FIG. 2.7.   Figure 2.6 repeated, but with the WSFACTORS subcommand continued on a second line.

The same principle applies when a repeated measures factor has more than two levels. For example, with three levels of A and two for B, the following set of labels for the six levels,

```
A1B1  A2B1  A3B1  A1B2  A2B2  A3B2,
```

would imply that B changes more slowly, while

```
A1B1  A1B2  A2B1  A2B2  A3B1  A3B2
```

would imply that A changes more slowly.

Continuing Commands and Subcommands on Another Line

Note that in Fig. 2.6, in two instances, a command's specifications were continued on the following line. When a command or its specifications are too long for a line, it is continued on the next line after having been indented at least one space on the continuing line. The principle is the same for subcommands, recognizing that subcommands begin at the fourth space. Therefore, if a subcommand has to be continued on another line, it begins at the fifth space (to accomodate the one space indentation). No slash would precede the continuing line, so the continuing line would be two spaces in from the slash in the preceding line (under the V in MANOVA), as illustrated in Fig. 2.7, with the continuation of the WSFACTORS subcommand onto a second line.

MIXED DESIGNS

Mixed designs are designs that include more than one factor, with at least one within subjects (repeated measures) factor, and at least one between subjects factor. The presence of a repeated measures factor requires the use of the MANOVA command. The only difference between a mixed and a repeated measures design, is in the need to specify the between subjects factor(s). The reader of this section should be familiar with the preceding material in this chapter concerning repeated measures factors.

To help in this discussion, the first four program statements from Figs. 2.2a and 2.4, which offer programs for repeated measures with one and two factors, respectively, are restated below:

```
TITLE ONE FACTOR REPEATED MEASURES A/V
DATA LIST LIST/A1 A2 A3
MANOVA A1 A2 A3
   /WSFACTORS = A(3)


TITLE TWO FACTOR REPEATED MEASURES A/V
DATA LIST LIST/A1B1 A1B2 A2B1 A2B2
MANOVA A1B1 A1B2 A2B1 A2B2
   /WSFACTORS = A(2) B(2)
```

These excerpts from the repeated measures programs illustrate how the repeated measures are given names in the WSFACTORS subcommand, where the numbers of levels are indicated in parentheses. In addition, if there is only one repeated measures factor, the individual levels of the factor are each given names in two places: the DATA LIST command, where the columns of numbers are first named (for example, A1 A2 A3), thus identifying the levels of the factor; and the MANOVA command, where the same names for each level are repeated. If there is more than one repeated measures factor, the levels of both factors are combined to offer a single set of levels for all repeated measures (for example, A1B1 A1B2 A2B1 A2B2), which also appears in two places (the DATA LIST and MANOVA command lines). There is a similar process of combining levels from separate factors when dealing with three or more repeated measures factors.

If a between subjects factor is added to the design, where is it placed and identified within the program? It appears in two places. It is placed adjacent to the levels of the repeated measures in the DATA LIST and MANOVA commands. Here we will follow the practice of always placing the labels for the between subjects factors immediately after the slash in the DATA LIST command, as in the following example where A is a between subjects factor and B is a repeated measure.

```
DATA LIST LIST/A B1 B2 B3
```

This statement suggests four columns of numbers in the presentation of data, where the first column will indicate the level of the between subjects factor, and the remaining three columns offer the actual data. That is, in column two, the scores for subjects under treatment condition (or measurement opportunity) B1, will appear; in column three, the B2 scores will be found, etc.

Another example, in which there is one between subjects factor A, and two repeated measures factors B and C, each with two levels, would have a DATA LIST command that looks like the following:

```
DATA LIST LIST/A BlCl BlC2 B2Cl B2C2
```

This second example suggests five columns in the presentation of the data, where again the first column will indicate the levels of the between subjects factor, while the remaining columns will contain the scores. For example, column two will contain the scores of subjects who were jointly affected by both level one of the B factor, and level one of the C factor, at the time of this measurement. Another score from the same subject would be found in column three, taken at the point in time when the subject was jointly affected by level one of B and level two of C. (If the data are presented in some other order, where the between subjects factor information was placed in some column other than the first, then this different order would have to be duplicated in the DATA LIST command, although it would not affect the order in the MANOVA command.)

The second place where information about the between subjects factor is placed is within the MANOVA command, but here it invariably *follows* the levels of the repeated measures, separated from them with the use of the keyword BY as illustrated in the following examples:

```
MANOVA Bl B2 B3 BY A(1,3)
```

or

```
MANOVA BlCl BlC2 B2Cl B2C2 BY A(1,3)
```

Note that the levels of the between subjects factor are indicated as in an ANOVA design (that is, using two numbers enclosed in parentheses). The above examples of the MANOVA command suggest three levels for the between subjects factor, with A(1,3).

If there is more than one between subjects factor, it is convenient to place them sequentially, preceding the levels of the repeated measures in the DATA LIST command, assuming that that is the way the data is organized. In the MANOVA command, the between subjects factors follow the repeated measures and the keyword BY on the MANOVA command line, as seen in the following example:

```
TITLE FOUR FACTOR A/V, TWO REPEATED MEASURES (C,D)
DATA LIST LIST/A B C1D1 C1D2 C1D3 C2D1 C2D2 C2D3
MANOVA C1D1 C1D2 C1D3 C2D1 C2D2 C2D3 BY A(1,2) B(1,4)
   /WSFACTORS=C(2) D(3)
```

The remainder of the program statements for designs involving both repeated measures and between subjects factors are identical to the programs
that involve only repeated measures factors.

Figures 2.8, 2.9, and 2.10 present three sample programs for three mixed
designs: A two factor design with one repeated measure, a three factor

```
TITLE TWO FACTORS WITH ONE REPEATED MEASURE (B)
DATA LIST LIST/A B1 B2 B3
MANOVA B1 B2 B3 BY A(1,3)
   /WSFACTORS = B(3)
   /PRINT = CELLINFO(MEANS)
   /DESIGN
BEGIN DATA
1 1 1 2
1 1 3 4
1 2 2 6
1 2 4 6
2 1 3 5
2 2 4 8
2 4 5 7
2 4 5 7
3 3 6 7
3 3 5 6
3 4 7 9
3 5 8 10
END DATA
```

FIG. 2.8. SPSS program for a two factor design with one repeated measure (B). There
are four subjects at each level of the between subjects factor.

```
TITLE THREE FACTORS WITH ONE REPEATED MEASURE (C)
DATA LIST LIST/A B C1 C2 C3
MANOVA C1 C2 C3 BY A(1,2) B(1,2)
   /WSFACTORS = C(3)
   /PRINT = CELLINFO(MEANS)
   /DESIGN
BEGIN DATA
1 1 1 2 3
1 1 2 3 4
1 1 3 4 5
1 1 2 2 6
1 2 2 3 7
1 2 3 4 8
1 2 4 5 7
1 2 3 5 8
2 1 3 4 8
2 1 4 5 9
2 1 5 5 9
2 1 6 6 8
2 2 5 8 10
2 2 6 9 12
2 2 7 9 11
2 2 7 6 12
END DATA
```

FIG. 2.9. SPSS program for a three factor design with one repeated measure (C).
There are four subjects in each cell (that is, in each combination of levels of factors A
and B).

```
TITLE THREE FACTORS WITH TWO REPEATED MEASURES (B,C)
DATA LIST LIST/A B1C1 B1C2 B2C1 B2C2
MANOVA B1C1 B1C2 B2C1 B2C2 BY A(1,2)
  /WSFACTORS=B(2) C(2)
  /PRINT=CELLINFO(MEANS)
  /DESIGN
BEGIN DATA
1 1 4 2 5
1 2 5 1 4
1 3 6 3 7
1 2 4 2 4
1 3 6 3 5
2 3 7 4 8
2 4 8 4 9
2 3 9 3 9
2 4 7 5 7
2 5 8 4 8
END DATA
```

FIG. 2.10. SPSS program for a three factor analysis of variance with two repeated measures (B and C). There are five subjects at each level of the between subjects factor (A).

design with one repeated measure, and a three factor design with two repeated measures. Data are included with each program, presented in each instance in the LIST data format. Note how, in Fig. 2.8, the first column is used to specify the level of the between subjects factor, and how, in Fig. 2.9, *both* the first *and* second column are used to specify the levels of the two between subjects factors.

Summary of Extrapolation to More Factors

For designs with more factors, simply place the additional factors in the statements in keeping with whether they are between subjects or within subjects (repeated measures) factors. The statements relevant to expanding the designs are summarized below:

1. In the MANOVA command line, the between subjects factors are placed *after* the word BY, which *follows* the levels of the within subjects factors.
2. The within subjects factors (as differentiated from the levels of the within subjects factors) are listed in the WSFACTORS command.
3. Numbers of levels of within subjects factors are stated in the WSFACTORS command line in parentheses, for example C(3), and number of levels of between subjects factors are implied in the MANOVA command line, also in parentheses, but preceded by a 1 and a comma, as in A(1,3).
4. If there are multiple within subjects factors, be sure to list all the

within subjects factors in the WSFACTORS subcommand in the proper order; the slowest changing first and the fastest changing last.

5.   Make sure that all of the factors are named within the DATA LIST statement, following the slash, and duplicating the order in the data.

Unequal Cell Sizes

In analysis of variance with multiple factors, unequal cell sizes create problems in the interpretation of the results. For this reason, most experimenters try to maintain equal cell sizes. The preceding programs all assume equal n size. However, SPSS can do the analysis with unequal cell sizes. What is required, is the addition of another subcommand, METHOD, and one of its keywords and options, SSTYPE(SEQUENTIAL), that is,

```
METHOD = SSTYPE(SEQUENTIAL),
```

following the WSFACTORS subcommand. The default is METHOD = SSTYPE(UNIQUE), which offers the standard equal n analysis, and so that is what you get without requesting it. The SPSS User's guide describes other keywords and options for the METHOD subcommand.

CORRECTION FOR BIAS IN TESTS OF REPEATED MEASURES FACTORS

Analysis of variance with repeated measures factors can result in positively biased F tests, primarily due to heterogeneity of the variances of differences among pairs of treatment measures (pairs of levels of a repeated measures factor). A reasonable preliminary question is whether or not heterogeneity of the variances of differences is present. A test for this, the Mauchly sphericity test, is offered in the SPSS printout. If it is statistically significant, it suggests that the assumptions are violated. Unfortunately, problems, primarily involving the test's oversensitivity, reduce its practical value. Kesselman, Rogan, Mendoza, and Breen (1980) demonstrated, with the aid of Monte Carlo data, that no advantage was gained by incorporating the Mauchly sphericity test in the decision process.

If heterogeneity of the variances of differences is present, a multivariate analysis of such data avoids the positive bias, and so multivariate tests of repeated measures are offered in the SPSS printouts. (Heterogeneity of the variances of differences cannot occur with only two levels of a factor, which is why the multivariate analysis is not offered with only two levels of a repeated measure.) There is some possibility that a multivariate analysis of repeated measures could lead to negative bias, resulting in tests with reduced power (Huynh & Feldt, 1976; Edwards, 1988). An alternative to the multivariate approach is the use of a correction in the degrees of freedom, permitting a choice of a larger critical F value, which, if properly selected, avoids the bias problem.

Box (1954) developed a correction factor, epsilon, a fractional value, which, if multiplied times both the numerator and denominator degrees of freedom of the F ratio, yields reduced degrees of freedom. The reduced degrees of freedom identify the correct (bias free) F distribution, which can then be used to obtain the correct critical F value for testing a repeated measures factor. The value of epsilon can serve both as a correction factor, and as a statement of the extent of the violation of the assumption of homogeneity of variances of differences. Epsilon varies between a value of 1 (no violation of the assumptions) and 1/(k-1) (maximum violation of the assumptions), where k is the number of levels of the repeated measures factor. The true epsilon is never known in actual data collection situations. Fortunately, there are two correction factors that are generally recognized as useful for estimating epislon: the Greenhouse–Geisser epsilon estimate (Greenhouse & Geisser, 1959); and the Huynh–Feldt epsilon estimate (Huynh & Feldt, 1976). Both epsilon estimates are given in the SPSS printout, when repeated measures are analyzed.

As suggested by the existence of a minimal value of epsilon, 1/k-1, reached under conditions of maximum violation of the assumptions, there is a limit to the extent of the bias effect. For example, if the degrees of freedom for an omnibus F test of a repeated measures factor with k levels, in a one factor repeated measures design, are (k-1), (n-1)(k-1), then the maximum violation, requiring that the degrees of freedom be multiplied by 1/(k-1), would result in the new smaller degrees of freedom of 1, (n-1). Greenhouse and Geisser (1959), using this recognition of a lower bound, suggested a procedure for conducting tests when univariate analysis of variance is used with repeated measures, and their suggestion has been endorsed by others in the field (e.g., Keppel, 1982; Myers, 1979).

Following their suggested procedure involves first checking the printout for the univariate F test of the repeated measures factor. If this test, which might be positively biased, is not statistically significant, the issue ends there, with no statistical significance. If however, the ordinary univariate F test leads to statistical significance, a more conservative test is tried. The printout, in the same table giving the Greenhouse–Geisser and Huynh–Feldt epsilon estimates, gives the lower bound epsilon. The researcher would multiply this lower bound epsilon times the degrees of freedom, and then use the resulting lower bound degrees of freedom to identify a new criterion F value in the F table. The empirical F would then be tested against this possibly conservative criterion. If the result is signficant even with the conservative criterion, then once again the issue is ended (this time with a conclusion of statistical significance). If the two tests contradict each other, that is, the positively biased test yields statistical significance, and the conservative (negatively biased) test does not, then a more specific epsilon correction in the degrees of freedom is made, in place of the lower bound correction.

The lower bound correction involves multiplication of the degrees of freedom by 1/(k-1), whereas the Greenhouse–Geisser or Huynh–Feldt epsilon estimates are likely to be larger, reaching 1/(k-1) only as a limit. The use of one of these estimates, besides being likely to yield more degrees of freedom, should yield degrees of freedom for the unbiased F distribution, the distribution that is more likely to represent the true degrees of freedom created by the extent of the violation of assumptions. The new degrees of freedom obtained with one of the estimates should then be used to select a new critical F value, with which a final statistical decision is made.

The next issue is the choice of the epsilon estimate. Huynh and Feldt (1976) recommended that their epsilon estimate should be used in most situations, reserving the Greenhouse–Geisser epsilon estimate for use only when the assumptions are strongly violated (when the true epsilon is less than .5). However, the true epsilon value is never known. If the two estimates are close, with both estimates low, one would be justified in using the Greenhouse–Geisser estimate. If both are high, the Huynh–Feldt estimate would be appropriate. If they contradict each other, one high and one low, there would be two different sets of degrees of freedom, which can be used to select a critical F value. In this case it might be useful to try both epsilons, testing the empirical F against the two different tabled critical F values. It would then be appropriate to use a decision procedure analogous to the one used with the lower bound degrees of freedom correction, and the F test with the original degrees of freedom. In this case the two different critical values will be closer together than when using the lower bound epsilon, improving the probabilities of the two epsilons leading to the same decision. If the two estimates lead to different decisions, this fact might simply be reported in the literature.

The procedure for using any of the three epsilons (the lower bound epsilon, the Greenhouse–Geisser epsilon, or the Huynh–Feldt epsilon), is the same. You multiply the chosen epsilon times both the numerator and denominator degrees of freedom. Since noninteger values of degrees of freedom can occur as the products, it is reasonable to round to the nearest integer. For example, assuming a two factor design with a repeated measures factor B containing three levels, and a between subjects factor A containing four levels, and ten subjects in each cell, the omnibus F test for B would have 2,72 df. The lower bound epsilon, displayed in the printout, would be .50. Multiplying this decimal value times 2 and 72 would yield degrees of freedom of 1,36. If the Huynh–Feldt epsilon was selected from the printout, and was found to be, say .68, the resulting degrees of freedom would be 1,49.

The F tables would be consulted for the new critical values of the adjusted degrees of freedom. The empirical F ratio would be tested against the new critical value. For 2,72 df, the critical value for a .05 Type I error probability, is 3.13; for 1,36 df, it is 4.11. A more specific estimate, such as the hypothetical Huynh–Feldt estimate of .68 which resuts in 1,49 df, yields a critical vallue between the other two, of 4.04.

READING THE PRINTOUTS FOR OMNIBUS F TESTS

The SPSS program you have entered appears early in the printout, minus JCL (job control language) statements, and usually minus data and the BEGIN DATA and END DATA commands. The descriptive information appears first, followed by the analysis of variance, often in several different tables, as explained below.

Exclusively Repeated Measures Factors

Immediately following the program you will find information about any possible missing data that caused subjects to be omitted. Immediately following this information will be the descriptive information and finally the significance tests.

Descriptive Information.   For a single factor repeated measures design, the means, standard deviations, n*s*, and 95% confidence intervals are given, for the criterion values at each level of the factor. This information appears in contiguous minitables divided by dotted lines, the first one beginning with a two line heading CELL MEANS AND STANDARD DEVIA-TIONS, and each table designating a level of the factor. The program in Fig. 2.2a of this chapter would yield a table which looks like Fig. 2.11.

Ignore the phrase FOR ENTIRE SAMPLE, which appears on the line with the mean, and which is explained in the context of mixed designs, in which it has meaning.

If there are two repeated measures factors, then the same descriptive information is given for the cells, each cell defined by the levels of the two

```
CELL MEANS AND STANDARD DEVIATIONS
VARIABLE . . Al
```

	MEAN	STD. DEV.	N . . .
FOR ENTIRE SAMPLE	3.75000	1.50000	4 . . .

FIG. 2.11.   Left side of first descriptive table produced by the program in Fig. 2.2a of this chapter.

factors. Thus, for two repeated measures factors A and B, there would be information on the mean, standard deviation, etc., for cells A1B1, A1B2, etc., so the descriptive information would begin with a table labeled

```
CELL MEANS AND STANDARD DEVIATIONS
VARIABLE . . A1B1 .
```

Analysis of Variance Summary Tables. The significance tests will be divided into two types, multivariate and univariate tests. The multivariate tests are only present when there are three or more levels of the repeated measures factor. With only two levels, only the univariate tests are done.

The multivariate tests in the SPSS printouts give three probability values, labeled PILLAIS, HOTTELINGS, and WILKS. They are each based on different formulas that are in common use, with no clear consensus as to which is best. However, they all tend to give answers that in most instances are quite close to one another. Generally, they are more conservative and give larger probability values than the traditional F ratio, although occasionally this will not be the case.

For each repeated measures factor a multivariate test precedes the univariate test, with the multivariate test clearly labeled as such. The univariate tests are labeled as "TESTS INVOLVING" —"WITHIN SUBJECT EFFECT," where the underlined space in quotes contains the name of the variable being test. Figure 2.12 offers an example of such a table. The within cells line in the table in Fig. 2.12 offers the error term, and the line with the factor name (in this example A) offers the sum of squares, mean squares, and significance level for the test of the factor.

Assuming that there are no between subjects factors in the design, the user may be surprised to find a table preceding the within subject variable tables, labeled "TESTS OF BETWEEN SUBJECTS EFFECTS." This table can be ignored for designs that lack between subjects factors.

A table that is similar to that seen in Fig. 2.12 will be found for the other repeated measures factor, and a third table for the interaction between the two. Different tables are provided for those sources of variance which use different error terms.

```
TESTS INVOLVING ''A'' WITHIN SUBJECT EFFECT

TESTS OF SIGNIFICANCE FOR T2 USING UNIQUE SUMS OF SQUARES
SOURCE OF VARIATION        SS       DF       MS         F       SIG OF F

WITHIN CELLS              .50        2      .25
A                       12.00        1    12.00      48.00         .020
```

FIG. 2.12. Example of a table giving a univariate F test of Factor A, in a two factor repeated measures design.

Mixed Designs

In mixed designs the initial sections of the printout are organized similarly
to the printouts for designs with exlusively repeated measures factors. That
is, they begin with information about any missing data that caused subjects
to be omitted, following this with the descriptive tables containing means,
and then finally offering the statistical tests.

Descriptive Information. For mixed designs, the same descriptive tables
that appear in exclusively repeated measures designs are further broken
down in terms of the levels of the between subjects factors. Thus, if examining a two factor mixed design, with one between subjects factor A,
containing three levels, and one repeated measures factor B, also containing three levels, the left hand side of the first minitable of descriptive
information would look like Fig. 2.13.

The word CODE in Fig. 2.13 refers to the level of the between subjects
factor. The phrase FOR ENTIRE SAMPLE is used to indicate that the
information refers to the level of the repeated measures factor without
regard to the between subjects factor. That is, for level B1 in Fig. 2.13,
the means are given at each level of factor A, and then, in the line designated FOR ENTIRE SAMPLE, the overall mean of B1 is given, across
all levels of A.

For mixed designs with more than one between subjects factor, the
levels of the between subjects factors are combined into cells defined by
all of the between subjects factors, yielding tables with the left side as seen
in Fig. 2.14, which offers an illustration for a three factor mixed design.
The top-most mean in Fig. 2.14, 2.00000, is the mean for the first levels
of A, B, and C, that is, A1B1C1. The second mean, 3.00000, is for cell
A1B2C1, and the third, 4.50000, is for A2B1C1.

Analysis of Variance Summary Tables. All of the information given in
the previous section on analysis of variance summary tables for exclusively

```
CELL MEANS AND STANDARD DEVIATIONS
VARIABLE . . B1
```

FACTOR	CODE	MEAN	STD. DEV.	. . .
A	1	1.50000	.57735	. . .
A	2	2.75000	1.50000	. . .
A	3	3.75000	.95743	. . .
FOR ENTIRE SAMPLE		2.66667	1.37069	. . .

FIG. 2.13. Left hand side of printout for a two factor mixed design (one repeated
measures factor, B), displaying some descriptive information. The remaining information (n, and confidence intervals), appears on the right of the table, but is omitted
here.

```
CELL MEANS AND STANDARD DEVIATIONS
VARIABLE . . C1

FACTOR                 CODE         MEAN              . . .


   A                    1
      B                 1        2.00000              . . .
      B                 2        3.00000              . . .

   A                    2
      B                 1        4.50000              . . .
      B                 2        6.250000             . . .

FOR ENTIRE SAMPLE                 3.93750  . . .
```

FIG. 2.14.   Left side of a descriptive table for the first level of C in a three factor design, with one repeated measures factor C. Factors A and B have two levels each.


```
TESTS INVOLVING ''B'' WITHIN-SUBJECT EFFECT.

AVERAGED TESTS OF SIGNIFICANCE FOR B USING UNIQUE SUMS OF SQUARES
SOURCE OF VARIATION          SS      DF      MS      F        SIG OF F

WITHIN CELLS               10.17     18      .56
B                          84.50      2    42.25    74.80       .000
A BY B                      4.00      4     1.00     1.77       .179
```

FIG. 2.15.   Example of a table in a two factor mixed design giving the univariate F tests of the within subjects factor, and its interaction with the between subjects factor.

repeated measures should be read before reading the remainder of this section. Some of the tables in the case of mixed designs will offer the tests for both the within subject factors, and their interactions with the between subjects factors, using the same labels and permitting the same interpretations as for the tables in the exclusively repeated measures designs. Figure 2.15 offers an example of one of the analysis of variance summary tables in a two factor mixed design; one which gives the tests of signficance for the repeated measures factor B, and its interaction with the between subjects factor A.

If the design contains more than one repeated measures factor, interactions with different repeated measures factors require different error terms. Thus, the WITHIN CELLS sources of variance will be different, for interactions with different repeated measures factors. SPSS includes only one WITHIN CELLS source of variance (one error term) within a single table. The result is that if there are multiple repeated measures factors, different tables will be used for their interactions with the between subjects factors. The sources of variance indicated within the tables will make clear which test results are present.

The tables for the univariate significance tests of the within subjects

```
TESTS OF BETWEEN-SUBJECTS EFFECTS.
TESTS OF SIGNIFICANCE FOR T1 USING UNIQUE SUMS OF SQUARES
SOURCES OF VARIATION          SS        DF        MS          F           SIG OF F

WITHIN CELLS                 38.83       9        4.31
CONSTANT                    729.00       1      729.00      168.95          .000
A                            63.50       2       31.75        7.36          .013
```

FIG. 2.16. Example of a table in a two factor mixed design giving the univariate test of a between subjects factor, A.

factors are preceded by the tables offering the analyses of the between subjects factors in tables titled TESTS OF BETWEEN-SUBJECTS EF-FECTS. As in the other tables the row headed WITHIN CELLS gives the error term. Figure 2.16 offers an example of such a table.

REFERENCES

Box, G. E. P. (1954). Some theorems on quadratic forms applied in the study of analysis of variance problems, II. Effect of inequality of variance and correlation between errors in the two way classification. *Annals of Mathematical Statistics, 25*, 484–498.

Edwards, L.K. (1988, April 28). *Multivariate methods aren't a cure-all for repeated measures designs*. Poster session abstract, Western Psychological Association meeting, San Francisco, CA.

Greenhouse, S. W., & Geisser, S. (1959). On methods in the analysis of profile data. *Psychometrika, 24*, 95–111.

Huynh, H., & Feldt, L. S. (1976). Estimation of the box correction for degrees of freedom from sample data in randomized block and split-plot designs. *Journal of Educational Statistics, 1*, 69–82.

Keppel, G. (1982). *Design and analysis: A researcher's handbook*. (2nd ed.). Englewood Cliffs, NJ: Prentice-Hall.

Kesselman, H. J., Rogan, J. C., Mendoza, J. L. & Breen, L. J. (1980). Testing the validity conditons of repeated measures. *Psychological Bulletin, 87*, 479–481.

Meyers, J. L. (1979). *Fundamentals of experimental design*. (3rd ed.). Boston: Allyn & Bacon.

3 Analysis of Covariance Programs

Analysis of covariance is a technique for removing some of the error variance associated with characteristics of individual subjects. Removing this same error variance from both the denominator and numerator of the F ratio increases the size of the ratio, making for a more powerful F test. The analysis of covariance is normally used only to remove this source of variability in "between subjects" factors and their error terms, although it can be used for repeated measures factors.

Analysis of covariance uses a covariate that is correlated with the dependent variable to reduce score variability. The degree of association between the covariate and the dependent variable is estimated, and then used to predict a subject's dependent variable score. The deviations from this predicted dependent measure are then used to compute the variances incorporated within the F test, in this way taking into account the covariate's association with the dependent variable. The use of a covariate can be expected to increase F values when the covariate is similarly distributed among the levels of the independent variable, since in this case the only effect of correcting for the covariate would be to decrease the error term. It can either increase or decrease the effects when the covariate is distributed differently over the levels of the independent variable. There are some questions about the interpretability of the results when there are large differences in the covariate among the levels of the independent variable.

Analysis of covariance for completely randomized designs can be done in SPSS with both the ANOVA and MANOVA commands, but not with the ONEWAY command. Doing analysis of covariance with the MANOVA command yields an estimate of the correlation between the covariate and the dependent variable, which is not provided in the printouts using the ANOVA command. Both types of programs are presented here for analysis of covariance with completely randomized designs. For mixed designs the MANOVA command must be used.

This chapter presents programs for one and two factor completely randomized designs; two factor designs with one between subjects factor; and three factor designs with both one and two between subjects factors. Extrapolation to designs with more variables is also discussed. The first program examined is a program for a one factor completely randomized design with a single covariate.

ONE FACTOR COMPLETELY RANDOMIZED DESIGN
WITH A COVARIATE

A sample program using ANOVA for a one factor completely randomized design, with a covariate, is illustrated in Fig. 3.1.

The data in Fig. 3.1 are contained in the second column, the first column indicating the levels of the factor. The third column offers the scores on the covariate. The factor in the program is labeled A and the dependent variable is referred to as SCORE. The covariate is labeled COV. All of these labels (A, SCORE, COV) are arbitrary and any other labels could be used.

In Fig. 3.1 the ANOVA command is used in line 3. Whether using

```
 1. TITLE ONE FACTOR CR DESIGN, WITH COVARIATE, ANOVA COMMAND
 2. DATA LIST LIST/A SCORE COV
 3. ANOVA SCORE BY A(1,3) WITH COV
 4.    /STATISTICS=MEAN
 5. BEGIN DATA
 6. 1 1 1
 7. 1 2 1
 8. 1 4 3
 9. 1 2 1
10. 1 2 2
11. 2 3 4
12. 2 4 3
13. 2 5 4
14. 2 5 3
15. 2 3 2
16. 3 4 5
17. 3 4 4
18. 3 6 4
19. 3 3 3
20. 3 3 2
21. END DATA
```

FIG. 3.1. Program for one factor CR design with a covariate, using the ANOVA command.

```
 1. TITLE ONE FACTOR CR DESIGN, WITH COVARIATE, MANOVA COMMAND
 2. DATA LIST LIST/A SCORE COV
 3. MANOVA SCORE BY A(1,3) WITH COV
 4.   /PRINT=CELLINFO(MEANS)
 5.   /DESIGN
 6. BEGIN DATA
 7. 1 1 1
 8. 1 2 1
 9. 1 4 3
10. 1 2 1
11. 1 2 2
12. 2 3 4
13. 2 4 3
14. 2 5 4
15. 2 5 3
16. 2 3 2
17. 3 4 5
18. 3 4 4
19. 3 6 4
20. 3 3 3
21. 3 3 2
22. END DATA
```

FIG. 3.2. Program for a one factor CR design with a covariate, using the MANOVA command.

ONEWAY, ANOVA, or MANOVA, the order of variables in the DATA LIST program statement (line 2) has to match the order of the columns in the data. In adding a covariate to a set of data, it is convenient to simply add a final column containing scores on the covariate, placing the label for the covariate last in the DATA LIST program statement. The order of the other variables that has been followed in this manual is factor (or factors) first, followed by the dependent variable. With the ANOVA command the order is dependent variable (here SCORE), followed by the keyword BY, followed by the factor (or factors) along with the number of levels indicated in parentheses, as seen in statement 3. The added presence of the keyword WITH signals that the next label is the label for the covariate (here COV). The subcommand and keyword

```
STATISTICS=MEAN
```

provides the means and sample sizes of the cells.

If the MANOVA command is used in place of the ANOVA command, two additional subcommands are needed. An example of such a program is presented in Fig. 3.2, which uses the same design and data as that presented in Fig. 3.1, but has MANOVA in place of ANOVA.

As usual with MANOVA, the last subcommand is DESIGN. The PRINT subcommand and its keywords provide for useful descriptive statistics. The analysis of covariance is requested through the keyword WITH in association with the MANOVA command, as seen in line 3 of Fig. 3.2.

TWO FACTOR COMPLETELY RANDOMIZED DESIGN WITH A COVARIATE

The program for a two factor completely randomized design with a covariate is almost identical to that for the one factor. The only difference is the added specification of the added factor. Figure 3.3 illustrates such a program with the ANOVA command and Fig. 3.4 illustrates such a program with the MANOVA command.

It should be clear from examining Figs. 3.1 and 3.3, or 3.2 and 3.4, that a covariance program can be altered to accommodate any number of between subjects factors by simply specifying more factors in the DATA LIST and MANOVA program statements.

TWO FACTOR DESIGN, ONE REPEATED MEASURE, WITH A COVARIATE

When doing an analysis of covariance with both between subjects and repeated measures factors, the full set of MANOVA subcommands are

```
1.  TITLE TWO FACTOR CR DESIGN WITH COVARIATE, ANOVA COMMAND
2.  DATA LIST LIST/A B SCORE COV
3.  ANOVA SCORE BY A(1,2) B(1,2) WITH COV
4.     /STATISTICS = MEAN
5.  BEGIN DATA
6.  1 1 3 1
7.  1 1 2 2
8.  1 1 3 2
9.  1 1 4 3
10. 1 1 3 1
11. 1 1 3 2
12. 1 2 5 2
13. 1 2 6 4
14. 1 2 7 4
15. 1 2 8 4
16. 1 2 5 2
17. 1 2 4 3
18. 2 1 1 2
19. 2 1 2 1
20. 2 1 3 3
21. 2 1 1 2
22. 2 1 3 4
23. 2 1 2 2
24. 2 2 7 6
25. 2 2 8 5
26. 2 2 8 7
27. 2 2 7 4
28. 2 2 9 3
29. 2 2 9 4
30. END DATA
```

FIG. 3.3. Program for a two factor CR design with a covariate, using the ANOVA command.

```
 1. TITLE TWO FACTOR CR DESIGN WITH COVARIATE, MANOVA COMMAND
 2. DATA LIST LIST/A B SCORE COV
 3. MANOVA SCORE BY A(1,2) B(1,2) WITH COV
 4.    /PRINT = CELLINFO(MEANS)
 5.    /DESIGN
 6. BEGIN DATA
 7. 1 1 3 1
 8. 1 1 2 2
 9. 1 1 3 2
10. 1 1 4 3
11. 1 1 3 1
12. 1 1 3 2
13. 1 2 5 2
14. 1 2 6 4
15. 1 2 7 4
16. 1 2 8 4
17. 1 2 5 2
18. 1 2 4 3
19. 2 1 1 2
20. 2 1 2 1
21. 2 1 3 3
22. 2 1 1 2
23. 2 1 3 4
24. 2 1 2 2
25. 2 2 7 6
26. 2 2 8 5
27. 2 2 8 7
28. 2 2 7 4
29. 2 2 9 3
30. 2 2 9 4
31. END DATA
```

FIG. 3.4. Program for two factor CR design with a covariate, using the MANOVA command and the necessary subcommands.

needed in order to deal with the repeated measures. This means adding the WSFACTORS subcommand. Another command is needed, and has to follow the DATA LIST command, but precede the MANOVA command. This is the COMPUTE command. It is repetitiously presented, with one such command for each level of the repeated measures factor. Thus, if there were three levels of a repeated measures factor, three uses of the COMPUTE command would be required. Specifically,

```
COMPUTE CV1 = COV
COMPUTE CV2 = COV
COMPUTE CV3 = COV
```

would appear as three separate program statements. This assumes that the covariate is labeled COV in the program.

The COMPUTE command is a transformation command, normally suggesting the creation of a new variable, say, from the sum of two others. However, it is used here to indicate that the covariate is always the same, across all levels of the repeated measures factor. (Although this is generally

```
 1. TITLE TWO FACTOR MIXED DESIGN, WITH COVARIATE
 2. DATA LIST LIST/A B1 B2 B3 COV
 3. COMPUTE CV1 = COV
 4. COMPUTE CV2 = COV
 5. COMPUTE CV3 = COV
 6. MANOVA B1 B2 B3 BY A(1,3) WITH CV1 CV2 CV3
 7.   /WSFACTORS = B(3)
 8.   /PRINT = CELLINFO(MEANS)
 9.   /DESIGN
10. BEGIN DATA
11. 1 1 1 2 1
12. 1 1 3 4 3
13. 1 2 2 6 2
14. 1 2 4 6 3
15. 2 1 3 5 3
16. 2 2 4 8 2
17. 2 4 5 7 4
18. 2 4 5 7 5
19. 3 3 6 7 3
20. 3 3 5 6 5
21. 3 4 7 9 3
22. 3 5 8 10 4
23. END DATA
```

FIG. 3.5. Program for a two factor design with one repeated measures factor and a covariate.

the case, it is possible to have the covariate vary across the levels of a repeated measure). The different names for the covariate are then used in the MANOVA command, which requires that a covariate be identified for each level of the repeated measure, and so the program requires several different names (although, as indicated in the COMPUTE commands, each individual subject has a single covariate). Figure 3.5 offers an example, in which the covariate names are CV1, CV2, and CV3.

THREE FACTOR DESIGN, TWO REPEATED MEASURES, WITH A COVARIATE

The program for a three factor design with two repeated measures is very similar to the program for a two factor design with one repeated measure. However, the total number of levels of all of the repeated measures has to be counted in deciding how many names are needed for the covariate. For example, with two levels of one repeated measure and three levels of another, there would be six repeated measurements, so six covariate labels would be needed. Six compute commands would be required to indicate that all six are equal to the same value for any individual subject. An example is given in Fig. 3.6, which includes two repeated measures factors that each has just two levels, requiring a total of four COMPUTE commands.

```
 1. TITLE THREE FACTORS, TWO REPEATED, WITH A COVARIATE
 2. DATA LIST LIST/A B1C1 B1C2 B2C1 B2C2 COV
 3. COMPUTE CV1 = COV
 4. COMPUTE CV2 = COV
 5. COMPUTE CV3 = COV
 6. COMPUTE CV4 = COV
 7. MANOVA B1C1 B1C2 B2C1 B2C2 BY A(1,2) WITH CV1 CV2 CV3 CV4
 8.   ·/WSFACTORS = B(2) C(2)
 9.    /PRINT = CELLINFO(MEANS)
10.    /DESIGN
11. BEGIN DATA
12. 1 1 4 2 5 1
13. 1 2 5 1 4 2
14. 1 3 6 3 7 2
15. 1 2 4 2 4 3
16. 1 3 6 3 5 4
17. 2 3 7 4 8 4
18. 2 4 8 4 9 3
19. 2 3 9 3 9 5
20. 2 4 7 5 7 4
21. 2 5 8 4 8 3
22. END DATA
```

FIG. 3.6. Program for a three factor design with two repeated measures and a co-variate.

THREE FACTOR DESIGN, ONE REPEATED MEASURE, WITH A COVARIATE

A covariance program for a three factor design with one repeated measure is again an extension of the previous variations introduced by a covariance analysis. The program is offered in Fig. 3.7.

EXTRAPOLATION TO DESIGNS WITH ADDITIONAL FACTORS

With more factors in the design, more factors have to be specified in the DATA LIST and MANOVA program statements. If there are additional repeated measures factors, or more levels of any repeated measures, this will influence the number of labels needed for the covariate, and affect the number of COMPUTE commands that are needed.

READING THE PRINTOUTS FOR ANALYSIS OF COVARIANCE PROGRAMS

If there are no repeated measures in the design there are two choices as to how to run the program, with ANOVA or with MANOVA. If ANOVA

```
 1. TITLE THREE FACTORS, ONE REPEATED, WITH A COVARIATE
 2. DATA LIST LIST/A B C1 C2 C3 COV
 3. COMPUTE CV1 = COV
 4. COMPUTE CV2 = COV
 5. COMPUTE CV3 = COV
 6. MANOVA C1 C2 C3 BY A(1,2) B(1,2) WITH CV1 CV2 CV3
 7.    /WSFACTORS = C(3)
 8.    /PRINT = CELLINFO(MEANS)
 9.    /DESIGN
10. BEGIN DATA
11. 1 1 1 2 3 1
12. 1 1 2 3 4 2
13. 1 1 3 4 5 3
14. 1 1 2 2 6 4
15. 1 2 2 3 7 4
16. 1 2 3 4 8 3
17. 1 2 4 5 7 4
18. 1 2 3 5 8 3
19. 2 1 3 4 8 4
20. 2 1 4 5 9 5
21. 2 1 5 5 9 3
22. 2 1 6 6 8 4
23. 2 2 5 8 10 3
24. 2 2 6 9 12 5
25. 2 2 7 9 11 4
26. 2 2 7 6 12 5
27. END DATA
```

FIG. 3.7. Program for a three factor design with one repeated measure and a covariate.

is used, the printout gives the summary of the analysis of covariance under the title ANALYSIS OF VARIANCE. Fig. 3.8 offers an example of such a table for a one factor analysis of covariance, using the data in Fig. 3.1 of this chapter. The principle information in the figure is in the line bearing the name of the independent variable (here A), where the probability of F is found. It is .619, so is not statistically significant. The error term is in the line headed RESIDUAL. The repetition of values in some lines is due to the fact that there is only one factor, so there is just one main effect. The MAIN EFFECTS LINE then simply repeats the results for A. When there is more than one factor, the same table includes the tests for the additional factors and interactions, and the MAIN EFFECTS line sums the sums of squares for the different factors.

When MANOVA is used for a completely randomized design, the table heading for the analysis of covariance is TESTS OF SIGNIFICANCE FOR [dependent variable] USING UNIQUE SUMS OF SQUARES, where the name of the dependent variable appears in place of the bracketed term. Figure 3.9 offers an example of such a table, using the same data as used for Fig. 3.8.

In Fig. 3.9 the important information is again in the line headed by the variable name (A in this example). The error term is found in the line

```
* * * ANALYSIS OF VARIANCE * * *
              SCORE
        BY   A
        WITH COV
```

SOURCE OF VARIATION	SUM OF SQURES	DF	MEAN SQUARE	F	SIGNIF OF F
COVARIATES	14.787	1	14.787	16.413	0.002
COV	14.787	1	14.787	16.413	0.002
MAIN EFFECTS	0.902	2	0.451	0.500	0.619
A	0.902	2	0.451	0.500	0.619
EXPLAINED	15.689	3	5.230	5.805	0.013
RESIDUAL	9.911	11	0.901		
TOTAL	25.600	14	1.829		

FIG. 3.8.   Analysis of covariance table for a one factor analysis of covariance design, computed with the ANOVA command.

```
* * * * * * * * * * ANALYSIS OF VARIANCE-DESIGN 1 * * * *
TESTS OF SIGNIFICANCE FOR SCORE USING UNIQUE SUMS OF SQUARES
```

SOURCE OF VARIATION	SS	DF	MS	F	SIG OF F
WITHIN CELLS	9.91	11	.90		
REGRESSION	4.89	1	4.89	5.43	.040
A	.90	2	.45	.50	.619

FIG. 3.9.   Analysis of variance table for a one factor analysis of covariance, computed with the MANOVA command.

headed WITHIN CELLS. The estimate of the correlation between the covariate and the dependent variable is given in a table below the TESTS OF SIGNIFICANCE TABLE, this other table bearing the title INDIVIDUAL UNIVARIATE .9500 CONFIDENCE INTERVALS. An example, from the same printout, is seen in Fig. 3.10.

Figure 3.10 offers the slope of the relationship between the covariate (on the X axis) and the dependent variable (on the Y axis), as computed from raw scores, calling it B. The same table offers a BETA value, which refers to the same relationship as B, but is computed with standardized scores. Using standardized scores in the computation of BETA makes BETA equivalent to the correlation between the covariate and the dependent variable. A t test of this correlation is also given in the table, and is seen, in Fig. 3.10, to have a significance value of .040. It is this correlation that is tested in the REGRESSION line of the TESTS OF SIGNIFICANCE table, seen in Fig. 3.9 (where again the significance value is found

```
----INDIVIDUAL UNIVARIATE .9500 CONFIDENCE INTERVALS
DEPENDENT VARIABLE . . SCORE
COVARIATE           B      BETA    STD ERR.    T-VALUE    SIG. OF T     . . .

COV              .661     .575       .284       2.330        .040       . . .
```

FIG. 3.10.   Table giving the slope of the dependent variable on the covariate (B), plus the correlation between the two (BETA), as well as a test of the significance of the correlation between the dependent variable and the covariate. Also appearing in the far right of the table (not shown here) are the 95% confidence intervals for the estimated correlation. (Most of the values in the actual table are given to ten decimal places.)

to be .040). The table in Fig. 3.10, in keeping with its heading (INDIVIDUAL UNIVARIATE .9500 CONFIDENCE INTERVALS), also gives the 95% confidence intervals for the estimated correlation.

When there are some repeated measures in the design, additional tables will be found giving the regular analysis of variance for the main effects of these within subjects factors and their interactions (including their interactions with the between subjects factors). These latter tables are all similar to those of a regular analysis of variance described in the preceding chapter, and are similarly labeled (TESTS INVOLVING 'B' WITHIN—SUBJECT EFFECT, for example).

When there are repeated measures in the design, and the COMPUTE command is used in the manner described previously, the printout will give a warning concerning a linearly dependent matrix and a resulting loss of degrees of freedom. This is a result of the special way in which the program has to be written (with the repetition of the COMPUTE command indicating that every level of the covariate on the repeated measure is equal to the same single variable). The loss of degrees of freedom specified in the warning does not actually affect the program in any way of concern to the user. The warning should simply be ignored.

4 Simple Effects Programs

For a simple effects test at least two factors are needed in the design. For example, the simple effects of factor A can be obtained with an omnibus F test at one or more preselected levels of factor B, or the simple effects of B can be obtained with an omnibus F test at one or more preselected levels of A. A simple effects test is generally done after a statistically significant interaction test. However, rather than running two programs, it may be convenient to include a simple effects test in the original program, when a statistically significant interaction is expected. If the interaction effect is not statistically significant, the simple effects tests should simply be ignored.

SIMPLE EFFECTS IN A MULTIFACTOR COMPLETELY RANDOMIZED DESIGN

The ANOVA command is normally used when working with multifactor completely randomized designs. However, in SPSS the simple effects programs are only available on MANOVA. MANOVA is therefore used for simple effects tests, even when there are no repeated measures factors present in the design. When working with a completely randomized design within the context of MANOVA, the MANOVA command is used in a program statement that has the same form as when using the ANOVA command; that is, the label for the dependent variable precedes the labels for the factors; and the keyword BY separates the dependent variable from the factors. Assuming a two factor completely randomized design, where both factors (labeled as A and B) have two levels, and the dependent variable is labeled SCORE, the MANOVA command would look like the following:

```
MANOVA SCORE BY A(1,2) B(1,2)
```

The DATA LIST program statement, as usual, would have the sequence of labels corresponding to the left to right order of the data. Given the practice in this manual of indicating factor level membership on the left, and actual scores to the right, the DATA LIST statement would look like the following:

```
DATA LIST LIST/A B SCORE
```

Thus the MANOVA and DATA LIST program statements reverse the order of factors and dependent variables (scores). Figure 4.1 illustrates a simple effects program within a two factor completely randomized design,

```
 1. TITLE TWO FACTOR COMPLETELY RANDOMIZED DESIGN
 2. SUBTITLE SIMPLE EFFECTS OF A AT LEVELS 1 AND 2 OF B
 3. DATA LIST LIST/A B SCORE
 4. MANOVA SCORE BY A(1,2) B(1,2)
 5.    /PRINT = CELLINFO(MEANS)
 6.    /DESIGN = A WITHIN B(1) A WITHIN B(2)
 7. BEGIN DATA
 8. 1 1 3
 9. 1 1 2
10. 1 1 3
11. 1 1 4
12. 1 1 3
13. 1 1 3
14. 1 2 5
15. 1 2 6
16. 1 2 7
17. 1 2 8
18. 1 2 5
19. 1 2 4
20. 2 1 1
21. 2 1 2
22. 2 1 3
23. 2 1 1
24. 2 1 3
25. 2 1 2
26. 2 2 7
27. 2 2 8
28. 2 2 8
29. 2 2 7
30. 2 2 9
31. 2 2 9
32. END DATA
```

FIG. 4.1. Two factor completely randomized design, requesting simple effects of A at levels 1 and 2 of B.

using the MANOVA command, and introduces the new statements needed for a simple effects test. These statements are added specifications to the DESIGN subcommand, in statement 6 in Fig. 4.1.

The actual simple effects request is made in the DESIGN subcommand, with rather direct specifications:

```
A WITHIN B(1) A WITHIN B(2) .
```

If you wish to compute the simple effects of B at each level of A, simply reverse the terms in the DESIGN subcommand, asking for B WITHIN A(1), etc.

Including the Main Effects and Interaction Tests

The program as given in Fig. 4.1 will only provide simple effects tests. That is, the added specifications in the DESIGN subcommand narrow the focus of the analysis. If, in addition, you also want the usual main effects and interactions for a two factor completely randomized design, you must add the DESIGN subcommand one more time, without any specifications. The DESIGN subcommand without specifications can either follow or precede the one with specifications. The program in Fig. 4.2 illustrates this fuller analysis.

More Than Two Factors in a Completely Randomized Design

When there are more than two factors, the simple effects of one factor at individual levels of another factor are requested in precisely the same way as with just two factors; the third factor is simply not referred to in the DESIGN subcommand requesting simple effects. Of course, the rest of the program does have the appropriate references to the third factor, as in the DATA LIST and MANOVA commands for the MANOVA version

```
1. TITLE TWO FACTOR COMPLETELY RANDOMIZED, PLUS SIMPLE EFFECTS
2. SUBTITLE A AT LEVELS 1 AND 2 OF B, PLUS MAIN EFFECTS
3. DATA LIST LIST/A B SCORE
4. MANOVA SCORE BY A(1,2) B(1,2)
5.   /PRINT = CELLINFO(MEANS)
6.   /DESIGN
7.   /DESIGN = A WITHIN B(1) A WITHIN B(2)
8. BEGIN DATA
   .
   .
   .
```

FIG. 4.2.   Two factor completely randomized design, requesting simple effects of A at levels 1 and 2 of B, plus the main effects and interaction.

of a three factor completely randomized design where each of the factors has two levels:

```
DATA LIST LIST/A B C SCORE

MANOVA SCORE BY A(1,2) B(1,2) C(1,2)
```

The request for the simple effects of A at level 1 of B,

```
/DESIGN = A WITHIN B(1)
```

would yield a test of whether the means of the different levels of A, each computed only at the first level of B, are different than each other. The scores contributing to each level of A in this test would include all of the scores at all levels of C. If there were two levels of A, and two levels of C, the two means computed and compared in the simple effects test of A at the first level of B would be computed from the scores summed over the two cells A1B1C1 and A1B1C2, and from the scores summed over the two cells A2B1C1 and A2B1C2.

Simple Simple Effects in a Completely Randomized Design.   Sometimes there is interest in the simple effect of A, at the first level of B, within only the first level of C (frequently called a simple simple effect). This could be tested by having the specification in the DESIGN subcommand as follows:

```
/DESIGN = A WITHIN B(1) WITHIN C(1)
```

Additional simple simple effects can be requested in the same DESIGN subcommand, as in

```
/DESIGN = A WITHIN B(1) WITHIN C(1) A WITHIN B(2) WITHIN C(1).
```

which requests the simple simple effects of A, within the first *and* second levels of B, both restricted to the first level of C.

SIMPLE EFFECTS IN A TWO FACTOR REPEATED MEASURES DESIGN

Where the requests for simple effects with between subjects factors are made in the DESIGN subcommand, the request for simple effects with repeated measures factors are made in another MANOVA subcommand, WSDESIGN. Just as the DESIGN subcommand uses specifications to restrict the analysis of between subjects factors, the WSDESIGN subcommand uses specifications to restrict the analysis of within subjects (repeated measures) factors.

When the WSDESIGN subcommand is not specified, it is implicitly present, as a default within the MANOVA program, calling for main effect and interaction analyses involving the within subjects factors. It could therefore be entered overtly as a subcommand, or omitted, with the same results, provided that what is desired is an unrestricted analysis of the repeated measures factors. When it is overtly entered as a subcommand, but, through particular keywords it calls for a more restricted analysis (such as simple effects tests), this takes precedence over the default that calls for a fuller analysis. This can cause problems in complex programs where several different analyses are called for. It is possible for one part of the program to require a full factorial analysis (that is, all main effects and interactions), but to have this contradicted by a restricted WSDESIGN subcommand in another part of the program. The program then might not run. This problem is most easily avoided by including an unrestricted WSDESIGN subcommand, following a WSFACTORS subcommand, but preceding a DESIGN subcommand, somewhere in the program. Then, restrictive specifications on the WSDESIGN subcommand that are found elsewhere in the program will not prevent the program from running. The program will recognize that both a full factorial analysis and some simple effects tests are being called for. Figure 4.3 offers an illustration of a simple effects request in a two factor repeated measures design, where the simple effects request appears on line 9.

In Fig. 4.3 the second WSDESIGN subcommand with the simple effects request is placed after the first DESIGN subcommand, on line 9. It is preceded by the unrestricted WSDESIGN subcommand on line 7. If in fact the full analysis of main effects was not desired, the WSDESIGN subcommand with the restrictions, as seen on line 9, could have been placed

```
 1.  TITLE TWO FACTORS REPEATED MEASURES DESIGN
 2.  SUBTITLE SIMPLE EFFECTS OF A AT LEVELS 1 AND 2 OF B
 3.  DATA LIST LIST/A1B1 A1B2 A2B1 A2B2
 4.  MANOVA A1B1 A1B2 A2B1 A2B2
 5.    /WSFACTORS = A(2) B(2)
 6.    /PRINT = CELLINFO(MEANS)
 7.    /WSDESIGN
 8.    /DESIGN
 9.    /WSDESIGN = A WITHIN B(1) A WITHIN B(2)
10.    /DESIGN
11.  BEGIN DATA
12.  1 3 2 6
13.  2 5 4 8
14.  4 5 5 7
15.  END DATA
```

FIG. 4.3. Two factor repeated measures design requesting simple effects of A at levels 1 and 2 of B, plus main effects and interaction.

on line 7, with the second WSDESIGN and DESIGN subcommands omitted from the program. The second DESIGN subcommand is included in Fig. 4.3 because the last subcommand following a MANOVA command must be the DESIGN subcommand.

More than Two Factors in a Repeated Measures Design

It is unusual to have more than two repeated measures in a single design. But if this were the case, and a simple effects test was needed, it would involve a simple extension of the two factor example. Specifically, the DATA LIST and MANOVA subcommands would incorporate the third factor in the labels for levels of the repeated measures. For example, with factors A, B, and C, each having two levels, the labels could be

```
A1B1C1 A1B1C2 A1B2C1 A1B2C2 A2B1C1 A2B1C2 A2B2C1 A2B2C2.
```

These labels would follow the slash in the DATA LIST program statement, and also follow the MANOVA command. The additional factor and its number of levels would be added to the WSFACTORS subcommand; following the order from changing most slowly to most quickly (discussed in Chapter Two in the section titled MULTIFACTOR REPEATED MEASURES DESIGNS). Here the order would be

```
/WSFACTORS = A(2) B(2) C(2).
```

The request for simple effects tests in the WSDESIGN subcommand would only mention the simple effects factor and the level of the factor at which it is being tested as in,

```
/WSDESIGN = A WITHIN B(1)
```

or

```
/WSDESIGN = B WITHIN C(1)
```

etc.

Simple Simple Effects in a Repeated Measures Design. A simple simple effect can be tested within a repeated measures design. Assuming three repeated measures factors A, B, and C, the WSDESIGN subcommand could include the following specifications:

```
/WSDESIGN = A WITHIN B(1) WITHIN C(1).
```

This would yield an omnibus F test of factor A at the first level of factor B within the first level of factor C.

SIMPLE EFFECTS TESTS WITH MIXED DESIGNS

When a single test of simple effects involves both a repeated measures factor and a between subjects factor, the keyword MWITHIN is used in place of the keyword WITHIN, to obtain a simple effects test. Secondly, both the DESIGN and WSDESIGN subcommands are used. The between subjects factor is named in the DESIGN subcommand, and the repeated measures factor is named in the WSDESIGN subcommand. Specifically, the request for a simple effects test of A at the first level of factor B, for example, would be broken into two parts, to be stated in two places. The factor for which the simple effects test is desired (A), being a between subjects factor, would be noted adjacent to the DESIGN subcommand, as in

```
/DESIGN = A.
```

The level of the second factor at which the simple effect is to be tested, B(1), is indicated adjacent to the WSDESIGN subcommand, along with the MWITHIN keyword, as in

```
/WSDESIGN = MWITHIN B(1).
```

In this way the combination of two subcommands,

```
/WSDESIGN = MWITHIN B(1)
/DESIGN = A
```

specifies the "mixed" simple effect (one involving both between and within subjects factors).

Stated another way, when A is a between subjects factor, B is a repeated measures factor, and A is the factor to be analyzed for the simple effect, factor A is noted in the DESIGN subcommand, while the level of the repeated measures factor at which the analysis is desired is noted in the preceding WSDESIGN subcommand, adjacent to the MWITHIN keyword.

The same placement of factor labels is used when testing the simple effect of the repeated measure (B). However, the keyword MWITHIN is moved to the DESIGN subcommand where the desired level of the between subjects variable is specified, as in, for example,

```
/DESIGN = MWITHIN A(1).
```

The two needed subcommands are then

```
/WSDESIGN=B
/DESIGN=MWITHIN A(1).
```

In summary, there are two possibilities for the request for a simple effects test involving one repeated measures factor and one between subjects factor. If A is the between subjects factor, and B is the repeated measures factor, the two subcommands would be either

```
/WSDESIGN=MWITHIN B(1)
/DESIGN=A
```

or

```
/WSDESIGN=B
/DESIGN=MWITHIN A(1),
```

depending on whether you wish to test the simple effect of A (the first case) or the simple effect of B (the second case). In both cases the repeated measures variable appears in the WSDESIGN subcommand, and the between subjects variable appears in the DESIGN subcommand.

It is possible to request the analysis of several levels within the same command. This is illustrated in Fig. 4.4, where the request for the simple

```
 1. TITLE TWO FACTORS WITH ONE REPEATED MEASURE (B)
 2. SUBTITLE SIMPLE EFFECTS OF FACTOR A
 3. DATA LIST LIST/A B1 B2 B3
 4. MANOVA B1 B2 B3 BY A(1,3)
 5.    /WSFACTORS=B(3)
 6.    /PRINT=CELLINFO(MEANS)
 7.    /WSDESIGN
 8.    /DESIGN
 9.    /WSDESIGN=MWITHIN B(1) MWITHIN B(2) MWITHIN B(3)
10.    /DESIGN=A
11. BEGIN DATA
12. 1 1 1 2
13. 1 1 3 4
14. 1 2 2 6
15. 1 2 4 6
16. 2 1 3 5
17. 2 2 4 8
18. 2 4 5 7
19. 2 4 5 7
20. 3 3 6 7
21. 3 3 5 6
22. 3 4 7 9
23. 3 5 8 10
24. END DATA
```

FIG. 4.4.   Two factor design with one repeated measure (B), requesting simple effects tests of factor A at levels 1, 2, and 3 of factor B, plus a full analysis.

```
 1.  TITLE TWO FACTORS WITH ONE REPEATED MEASURE (B)
 2.  SUBTITLE SIMPLE EFFECTS OF FACTOR B
 3.  DATA LIST LIST/A B1 B2 B3
 4.  MANOVA B1 B2 B3 BY A(1,3)
 5.    /WSFACTORS=B(3)
 6.    /PRINT=CELLINFO(MEANS)
 7.    /WSDESIGN
 8.    /DESIGN
 9.    /WSDESIGN=B
10.    /DESIGN=MWITHIN A(1) MWITHIN A(2) MWITHIN A(3)
11.  BEGIN DATA
12.  1 1 1 2
13.  1 1 3 4
14.  1 2 2 6
15.  1 2 4 6
16.  2 1 3 5
17.  2 2 4 8
18.  2 4 5 7
19.  2 4 5 7
20.  3 3 6 7
21.  3 3 5 6
22.  3 4 7 9
23.  3 5 8 10
24.  END DATA
```

FIG. 4.5. Two factor design with one repeated measure (B), requesting simple effects tests of factor B at levels 1, 2, and 3 of factor A, plus full analysis.

effects test on factor A indicates that the test is to be repeated at all three levels of factor B. It does this by including three MWITHIN keywords in the same WSDESIGN subcommand, each associated with a level of factor B.

Note that, in Fig. 4.4, the WSDESIGN and DESIGN subcommands specifying the requests for simple effects tests (lines 9 and 10), follow unrestricted WSDESIGN and DESIGN subcommands (lines 7 and 8), permitting a full analysis to be included with the simple effects tests.

In Fig. 4.5, which contains a program in which the simple effects of the repeated measures factor B are being tested at all levels of the between subjects factor (A), the several requests are once again repeated on one line, this time adjacent to the DESIGN subcommand (although the single factor specification is made adjacent to the WSDESIGN subcommand).

In summary, when both a repeated measures factor and a between subjects factor are involved in a simple effects test, the keyword MWITHIN is used in place of WITHIN. The name for the between subjects factor always appears with the DESIGN subcommand, and the name for the repeated measures factor always appears with the WSDESIGN subcommand. The name of the factor for which the simple effects are desired is placed alone adjacent to the appropriate subcommand (WSDESIGN or DESIGN), following an equals sign. The keyword MWITHIN is placed with the other subcommand, along with the levels of the second factor that are of interest.

More Than Two Factors in a Mixed Design

The programs for computing simple effects with more than two factors in a mixed design would follow the forms previously suggested. The third factor would simply not be mentioned in the simple effects analyses. Fig. 4.6 gives a program for a simple effects test of factor A at two levels of factor B, in a three factor design where there are two repeated measures, B and C. Since the test involves both a repeated measures factor and a between subjects factor (B and A respectively), the MWITHIN keyword is used, along with both the DESIGN and WSDESIGN subcommands for detailing the simple effects to be tested.

Figure 4.7 offers the converse of the program in Fig. 4.6, in requesting the simple effects of B at levels 1 and 2 of A. In this case the MWITHIN keyword is moved to the DESIGN subcommand.

Suppose the simple effects analysis of both B and C were desired, at both levels of A. In that case, the DESIGN subcommand would appear as usual, but the WSDESIGN subcommand would not have any specification,

```
/WSDESIGN
/DESIGN=MWITHIN A(1) MWITHIN(A2).
```

```
 1. TITLE THREE FACTORS WITH TWO REPEATED MEASURES, (B,C)
 2. SUBTITLE SIMPLE EFFECTS OF A AT LEVELS 1 AND 2 OF B
 3. DATA LIST LIST/A B1C1 B1C2 B2C1 B2C2
 4. MANOVA B1C1 B1C2 B2C1 B2C2 BY A(1,2)
 5.    /WSFACTORS=B(2) C(2)
 6.    /PRINT=CELLINFO(MEANS)
 7.    /WSDESIGN
 8.    /DESIGN
 9.    /WSDESIGN=MWITHIN B(1) MWITHIN B(2)
10.    /DESIGN=A
11. BEGIN DATA
12. 1 1 4 2 5
13. 1 2 5 1 4
14. 1 3 6 3 7
15. 1 2 4 2 4
16. 1 3 6 3 5
17. 2 3 7 4 8
18. 2 4 8 4 9
19. 2 3 9 3 9
20. 2 4 7 5 7
21. 2 5 8 4 8
22. END DATA
```

FIG. 4.6.   Three factor design with two repeated measures (B and C), requesting simple effects tests of factor A at levels 1 and 2 of B, plus a full analysis.

```
 1. TITLE THREE FACTORS WITH TWO REPEATED MEASURES, (B,C)
 2. SUBTITLE SIMPLE EFFECTS OF B AT LEVELS 1 AND 2 OF A
 3. DATA LIST LIST/A B1C1 B1C2 B2C1 B2C2
 4. MANOVA B1C1 B1C2 B2C1 B2C2 BY A(1,2)
 5.    /WSFACTORS=B(2) C(2)
 6.    /PRINT=CELLINFO(MEANS)
 7.    /WSDESIGN
 8.    /DESIGN
 9.    /WSDESIGN=B
10.    /DESIGN=MWITHIN A(1) MWITHIN A(2)
11. BEGIN DATA
12. 1 1 4 2 5
13. 1 2 5 1 4
14. 1 3 6 3 7
15. 1 2 4 2 4
16. 1 3 6 3 5
17. 2 3 7 4 8
18. 2 4 8 4 9
19. 2 3 9 3 9
20. 2 4 7 5 7
21. 2 5 8 4 8
22. END DATA
```

FIG. 4.7.   Three factor design with two repeated measures (B and C), requesting simple effects tests of factor B at levels 1 and 2 of A, plus full analysis.

In this case, the program would run the simple effects tests for both B and C at the specified levels of A. In fact, since the WSDESIGN subcommand would not have any restrictive specifications, it would not be necessary to include it, since the MANOVA program default is an unrestricted WSDESIGN subcommand. This means that the preceding WSDESIGN subcommand on line 9 in Fig. 4.7 could also be omitted. However, the instances in which the WSDESIGN subcommand can and can not be omitted might be confusing, so simply including it usually offers the safest way to proceed.

It is possible, within a mixed design containing three or more factors, to be dealing exclusively with only between subjects factors, or exclusively with repeated measures factors, in the simple effects test. For example, assume that what is desired is a simple effects test of a repeated measures factor at a couple of levels of another repeated measures factor, in a mixed three factor design, with variables B and C as the repeated measures factors. The simple effects program would mirror the program for a two factor design with only repeated measures. That is, only the WSDESIGN subcommand would be used, in conjunction with the WITHIN keyword, as seen in Fig. 4.8.

An analogous situation exists for two between subject variables in a three factor design with one repeated measure. For such a design the simple effect of a between subjects factor at some levels of the other between subjects factor could be obtained in the manner illustrated in Fig. 4.9.

In Fig. 4.9 there are no WSDESIGN subcommands, because there are

```
 1. TITLE THREE FACTORS WITH TWO REPEATED MEASURES B AND C
 2. SUBTITLE SIMPLE EFFECTS OF FACTOR B AT LEVELS 1 AND 2 OF C
 3. DATA LIST LIST/A B1C1 B1C2 B2C1 B2C2
 4. MANOVA B1C1 B1C2 B2C1 B2C2 BY A(1,2)
 5.    /WSFACTORS=B(2) C(2)
 6.    /PRINT=CELLINFO(MEANS)
 7.    /WSDESIGN
 8.    /DESIGN
 9.    /WSDESIGN=B WITHIN C(1) B WITHIN C(2)
10.    /DESIGN
11. BEGIN DATA
12. 1 1 4 2 5
13. 1 2 5 1 4
14. 1 3 6 3 7
15. 1 2 4 2 4
16. 1 3 6 3 5
17. 2 3 7 4 8
18. 2 4 8 4 9
19. 2 3 9 3 9
20. 2 4 7 5 7
21. 2 5 8 4 8
22. END DATA
```

FIG. 4.8.   Three factor design with two repeated measures (B and C), requesting simple effects tests of factor B at levels 1 and 2 of C, plus full analysis.

```
 1. TITLE THREE FACTORS WITH ONE REPEATED MEASURE (C)
 2. SUBTITLE SIMPLE EFFECTS OF FACTOR A AT LEVELS 1 AND 2 OF B
 3. DATA LIST LIST/A B C1 C2 C3
 4. MANOVA C1 C2 C3 BY A(1,2) B(1,2)
 5.    /WSFACTORS=C(3)
 6.    /PRINT=CELLINFO(MEANS)
 7.    /DESIGN
 8.    /DESIGN=A WITHIN B(1) A WITHIN B(2)
 9. BEGIN DATA
10. 1 1 1 2 3
11. 1 1 2 3 4
12. 1 1 3 4 5
13. 1 1 2 2 6
14. 1 2 2 3 7
15. 1 2 3 4 8
16. 1 2 4 5 7
17. 1 2 3 5 8
18. 2 1 3 4 8
19. 2 1 4 5 9
20. 2 1 5 5 9
21. 2 1 6 6 8
22. 2 2 5 8 10
23. 2 2 6 9 12
24. 2 2 7 9 11
25. 2 2 7 6 12
26. END DATA
```

FIG. 4.9.   Three factor design with one repeated measure (C), requesting simple effects tests of factor A at levels 1 and 2 of B, plus full analysis.

no restrictions needing to be placed on a WSDESIGN subcommand. There-fore the default WSDESIGN subcommand is implicitly present, permitting the full analysis. The restricted simple effects analysis that is also desired only involves between subjects factors. However, if a WSDESIGN sub-command, without any keywords, appeared preceding a DESIGN sub-command, it would be redundant with the default, and so would not have any effect.

Figure 4.10 offers an example of simple effects with mixed factors in a three factor design with only one repeated measures factor, C, where the simple effect of C is being tested at each of the levels of A.

For a test of the simple effects of A at all levels of C, the MWITHIN keyword would again be used, but moved to the WSDESIGN subcom-mand, as illustrated in Fig. 4.11.

Simple Effects of Several Factors and Selected Interactions

Figure 4.11 offers a three factor design with one repeated measure. It illustrates the request for the simple effects of one of the two between

```
 1. TITLE THREE FACTORS WITH ONE REPEATED MEASURE (C)
 2. SUBTITLE SIMPLE EFFECTS OF FACTOR C AT LEVELS 1 AND 2 OF A
 3. DATA LIST LIST/A B C1 C2 C3
 4. MANOVA C1 C2 C3 BY A(1,2) B(1,2)
 5.   /WSFACTORS = C(3)
 6.   /PRINT = CELLINFO(MEANS)
 7.   /WSDESIGN
 8.   /DESIGN
 9.   /WSDESIGN = C
10.   /DESIGN = MWITHIN A(1) MWITHIN A(2)
11. BEGIN DATA
12. 1 1 1 2 3
13. 1 1 2 3 4
14. 1 1 3 4 5
15. 1 1 2 2 6
16. 1 2 2 3 7
17. 1 2 3 4 8
18. 1 2 4 5 7
19. 1 2 3 5 8
20. 2 1 3 4 8
21. 2 1 4 5 9
22. 2 1 5 5 9
23. 2 1 6 6 8
24. 2 2 5 8 10
25. 2 2 6 9 12
26. 2 2 7 9 11
27. 2 2 7 6 12
28. END DATA
```

FIG. 4.10. Three factor design with one repeated measure (C), requesting simple effects tests of factor C at levels 1 and 2 of A, plus full analysis.

```
 1. TITLE THREE FACTORS WITH ONE REPEATED MEASURE (C)
 2. SUBTITLE SIMPLE EFFECTS OF A AT ALL LEVELS OF C
 3. DATA LIST LIST/A B C1 C2 C3
 4. MANOVA C1 C2 C3 BY A(1,2) B(1,2)
 5.   /WSFACTORS=C(3)
 6.   /PRINT=CELLINFO(MEANS)
 7.   /WSDESIGN
 8.   /DESIGN
 9.   /WSDESIGN=MWITHIN C(1) MWITHIN C(2) MWITHIN C(3)
10.   /DESIGN=A
11. BEGIN DATA
12. 1 1 1 2 3
13. 1 1 2 3 4
14. 1 1 3 4 5
15. 1 1 2 2 6
16. 1 2 2 3 7
17. 1 2 3 4 8
18. 1 2 4 5 7
19. 1 2 3 5 8
20. 2 1 3 4 8
21. 2 1 4 5 9
22. 2 1 5 5 9
23. 2 1 6 6 8
24. 2 2 5 8 10
25. 2 2 6 9 12
26. 2 2 7 9 11
27. 2 2 7 6 12
28. END DATA
```

FIG. 4.11. Three factor design with one repeated measures factor (C), requesting simple effects of factor A at all three levels of factor C, plus full analysis.

```
 .
 .
 .
 8.   /DESIGN
 9.   /WSDESIGN=MWITHIN C(1) MWITHIN C(2) MWITHIN C(3)
10.   /DESIGN
11. BEGIN DATA
 .
 .
 .
```

FIG. 4.12. Optional restatement of part of the program in Fig. 4.11 to obtain the simple effects of *both* variables A and B, along with the simple effect of their interaction.

subjects factors. What if the simple effects of both between subjects factors were desired? In that case, both factor names could be included with the second DESIGN subcommand on line 10 in Fig. 4.11, looking like

```
/DESIGN=A B .
```

If the simple effects of the interaction of A and B was also of interest, this too could be specified in the DESIGN subcommand, looking like

```
/DESIGN=A B A BY B .
```

In the case of the design in Fig. 4.11, where there are only two between subjects factors, there is a simpler way to proceed if both factors and their interaction were to be analyzed as simple effects. This would be to simply omit any specifications on either DESIGN subcommand. Figure 4.12 reproduces the relevant part of Fig. 4.11, with the needed changes. This omission of any specifications on a DESIGN subcommand even though a simple effect is requested with mixed factors, is part of a general principle. Given that there is an MWITHIN keyword and specifications on the WSDESIGN subcommand, an absence of any specification on a DESIGN subcommand will result in all of the between subjects factors in the design being analyzed with the simple effects suggested in the WSDESIGN subcommand.

An analogous procedure can be followed if simple effects are desired concerning all of the repeated measures factors at some specified levels of a between subjects factor, say in a three factor design with two repeated measures. In this case, the specified levels of the between subjects factor would follow the MWITHIN keyword on a DESIGN subcommand, but no repeated measures factors would be specified on a WSDESIGN subcommand.

Simple Simple Effects in a Mixed Design.   Assume a three factor design, A, B, and C, with two repeated measures, B and C. Further, assume that what is wanted is the simple simple effect of factor A at the first level of factor B, within the first level of factor C. The program would be the one illustrated in Fig. 4.13.

Note that MWITHIN is used as the first keyword in line 9 in Fig. 4.13 to tie the between subjects factor A named in the DESIGN subcommand to the repeated measures factor B named in the WSDESIGN subcommand.

```
 1. TITLE THREE FACTORS WITH TWO REPEATED MEASURES
 2. SUBTITLE SIMPLE SIMPLE EFFECT OF A AT B(1) WITHIN C(1)
 3. DATA LIST LIST/A B1C1 B1C2 B2C1 B2C2
 4. MANOVA B1C1 B1C2 B2C1 B2C2 BY A(1,2)
 5.    /WSFACTORS = B(2) C(2)
 6.    /PRINT = CELLINFO(MEANS)
 7.    /WSDESIGN
 8.    /DESIGN
 9.    /WSDESIGN = MWITHIN B(1) WITHIN C(1)
10.    /DESIGN = A
11. BEGIN DATA
        .
        .
        .
```

FIG. 4.13. Simple simple effect of factor A at level one of B within level one of C. (Two repeated measures.)

However, the WITHIN keyword is used to tie the two repeated measures factors (B & C) together within the same subcommand in line 9.

If more than one simple effect of A was being examined, the additional requests could follow on the same WSDESIGN subcommand, as seen in Fig. 4.14.

In a simple simple effect test three factors have to be mentioned. In a three factor mixed design they will not all be between subjects factors, or all repeated measures factors. The general principles to be observed are that the between subjects factors must appear in the DESIGN subcommand, and the repeated measures in the WSDESIGN subcommand. Further, the variable whose simple simple effects are being sought does not have any level specified, and is not preceded by any keyword. *Between* any two variables mentioned within one subcommand, the keyword used

```
 1. TITLE THREE FACTORS WITH TWO REPEATED MEASURES
 2. SUBTITLE SIMPLE SIMPLE EFFECTS OF A AT B(1) & B(2) WITHIN C(1)
 3. DATA LIST LIST/A B1C1 B1C2 B2C1 B2C2
 4. MANOVA B1C1 B1C2 B2C1 B2C2 BY A(1,2)
 5.    /WSFACTORS=B(2) C(2)
 6.    /PRINT=CELLINFO(MEANS)
 7.    /WSDESIGN
 8.    /DESIGN
 9.    /WSDESIGN=MWITHIN B(1) WITHIN C(1) MWITHIN B(2) WITHIN C(1)
10.    /DESIGN=A
11. BEGIN DATA
     .
     .
     .
```

FIG. 4.14. Simple simple effects of factor A at levels one and two of B within level one of C. (Two repeated measures).

```
 1. TITLE THREE FACTORS WITH TWO REPEATED MEASURES
 2. SUBTITLE SIMPLE SIMPLE EFFECT OF B AT C(1) WITHIN A(1)
 3. DATA LIST LIST/A B1C1 B1C2 B2C1 B2C2
 4. MANOVA B1C1 B1C2 B2C1 B2C2 BY A(1,2)
 5.    /WSFACTORS=B(2) C(2)
 6.    /PRINT=CELLINFO(MEANS)
 7.    /WSDESIGN
 8.    /DESIGN
 9.    /WSDESIGN=B WITHIN C(1)
10.    /DESIGN=MWITHIN A(1)
11. BEGIN DATA
     .
     .
     .
```

FIG. 4.15. Simple simple effect of factor B at the first level of C within the first level of A. (Two repeated measures.)

will be WITHIN, since they will both be between subjects factors, or both will be repeated measures factors. However, the keyword MWITHIN will precede one of the variable labels that has a level specified, on one of the lines, because it must be linked to a variable on another subcommand. In essence, the three variables must be linked by keywords, with MWITHIN linking a pair of mixed variables on two different lines, and WITHIN linking a pair of variables of the same class on the same line.

If one wanted the simple simple effect of repeated measures variable B within the first level of repeated measures variable C within the first level of between subjects variable A, the program would look like the one shown in Fig. 4.15.

The preceding examples all concern a three factor design with two repeated measures. Figures 4.16 and 17 offer two programs for simple simple effects in a three factor design with one repeated measure.

```
 1. TITLE THREE FACTORS WITH ONE REPEATED MEASURE (C)
 2. SUBTITLE SIMPLE SIMPLE EFFECTS OF A AT B(1) & B(2) WITHIN C(1)
 3. DATA LIST LIST/A B C1 C2 C3
 4. MANOVA C1 C2 C3 BY A(1,2) B(1,2)
 5.    /WSFACTORS = C(3)
 6.    /PRINT = CELLINFO(MEANS)
 7.    /WSDESIGN
 8.    /DESIGN
 9.    /WSDESIGN = MWITHIN C(1)
10.    /DESIGN = A WITHIN B(1) A WITHIN B(2)
11. BEGIN DATA
      .
      .
      .
```

FIG. 4.16. Simple simple effects of factor A at the first and second levels of factor B, within the first level of factor C. (One repeated measure.)

```
 1. TITLE THREE FACTORS WITH ONE REPEATED MEASURE (C)
 2. SUBTITLE SIMPLE SIMPLE EFFECTS OF C AT A(1) & A(2) WITHIN B(1)
 3. DATA LIST LIST/A B C1 C2 C3
 4. MANOVA C1 C2 C3 BY A(1,2) B(1,2)
 5.    /WSFACTORS = C(3)
 6.    /PRINT = CELLINFO(MEANS)
 7.    /WSDESIGN
 8.    /DESIGN
 9.    /WSDESIGN = C
10.    /DESIGN = MWITHIN A(1) WITHIN B(1) MWITHIN A(2) WITHIN B(1)
11. BEGIN DATA
      .
      .
      .
```

FIG. 4.17. Simple simple effects of factor C at the first and second levels of factor A, within the first level of factor B. (One repeated measure.)

```
* * * * * * * * * * * ANALYSIS OF VARIANCE -- DESIGN 2 * * * *

TESTS OF SIGNIFICANCE FOR SCORE USING UNIQUE SUMS OF SQUARES
SOURCE OF VARIATION            SS        DF           MS           F      SIG OF F

WITHIN CELLS                 74.83      45           1.66
A WITHIN B(1)                 4.00       2           2.00        1.20       .310
A WITHIN B(2)               146.33       2          73.17       44.00       .000
A WITHIN B(3)               161.78       2          80.89       48.64       .000
```

FIG. 4.18.   Simple effects of factor A within each of the three levels of factor B, in a two factor completely randomized design.

```
* * * * * * * * * * * ANALYSIS OF VARIANCE -- DESIGN 2 * * * *

TESTS OF SIGNIFICANCE FOR SCORE USING UNIQUE SUMS OF SQUARES
SOURCE OF VARIATION            SS        DF           MS           F      SIG OF F

WITHIN CELLS                 55.33      40           1.38
A WITHIN B(1) WITHIN          3.00       1           3.00        2.17       .149
  C(1)
A WITHIN B(1) WITHIN          1.33       1           1.33         .96       .332
  C(2)
```

FIG. 4.19.   Simple simple effects of factor A within the first level of factor B at the first and second levels of factor C, in a three factor completely randomized design.

```
* * * * * * * * * * * ANALYSIS OF VARIANCE -- DESIGN 2 * * * *

TESTS INVOLVING 'A WITHIN B(1)' WITHIN-SUBJECT EFFECT

TESTS OF SIGNIFICANCE FOR MEAS. 1 USING UNIQUE SUMS OF SQUARES
SOURCE OF VARIATION            SS        DF           MS           F      SIG OF F

WITHIN CELLS                 13.89      10           1.39
A WITHIN B(1)                69.44       2          34.72       25.00       .000
```

FIG. 4.20.   Simple effect of factor A within the first level of factor B in a two factor repeated measures design.

```
* * * * * * * * * * * ANALYSIS OF VARIANCE -- DESIGN 2 * * * * *
TESTS INVOLVING 'MWITHIN B(1)' WITHIN-SUBJECT EFFECT

TEST OF SIGNIFICANCE FOR T1 USING UNIQUE SUMS OF SQUARES
SOURCE OF VARIATION            SS         D           MS           F      SIG OF F

WITHIN CELLS                 10.50       9           1.17
MWITHIN B(1)                 85.33       1          85.33       73.14       .000
A BY MWITHIN B(1)            10.17       2           5.08        4.36       .047
```

FIG. 4.21.   Simple effect test of the between subject factor A at the first level of repeated measures factor B, in a two factor mixed design.

READING THE PRINTOUTS FOR SIMPLE EFFECTS PROGRAMS

The printouts for simple effects in a completely randomized design will have a heading TESTS OF SIGNIFICANCE FOR _____USING UNIQUE SUMS OF SQUARES where the empty space (here underlined) will contain the word for the dependent variable (SCORES in the examples in this manual). These tables will give the simple effects. Simple simple effects will also appear in tables with that heading. The error terms for the F ratios will always be on lines with the heading WITHIN CELLS. Figure 4.18 illustrates a printout of simple effects in a two factor completely randomized design, and Fig. 4.19 illustrates simple simple effects in a three factor completely randomized design.

In a design that only contains repeated measures the table headings are different, and separate tables are used for different simple effects of the same factor, because different error terms are used for each test. Figure 4.20 offers an example of a test of one of the simple effects in a two factor repeated measures design.

In mixed simple effects tests the word BY appears in the row headngs, although the tables are otherwise similar to the ones seen above. Figure 4.21 offers an example of a table for the simple effect of a between subjects factor, A, at the first level of a repeated measures factor, B, in a two factor mixed design. Figure 4.22 offers an example of a table for the simple effects of a repeated measures factor, B, at all three levels of the between subjects factor, A.

In Fig. 4.21 there is a line that should be ignored. This is the line with the line heading MWITHIN B(1). Any line heading that does not contain the name of a variable, but only the level of a variable, will not contain the desired simple effect test information. In some printouts a table will be present that only contains line headings that lack variable names, and so the entire table should be bypassed. The meaningful lines in tables are lines such as A WITHIN B(1), or A BY MWITHIN B(2), read as A within B(2), or MWITHIN A(1) BY B, read as B within A(1). Each of these

```
* * * * * * * * * * * ANALYSIS OF VARIANCE -- DESIGN 2 * * * * *
TESTS INVOLVING 'B' WITHIN-SUBJECT EFFECT
```

AVERAGED TESTS OF SIGNIFICANCE FOR B USING UNIQUE SUMS OF SQUARES

SOURCE OF VARIATION	SS	D	MS	F	SIG OF F
WITHIN CELLS	10.17	18	.56		
MWITHIN A(1) BY B	18.67	2	9.33	16.52	.000
MWITHIN A(2) BY B	32.67	2	16.33	28.92	.000
MWITHIN A(3) BY B	37.17	2	18.58	32.90	.000

FIG. 4.22. Simple effects tests of the repeated measures factor B at all three levels of the between subjects factor A, in a two factor mixed design.

```
* * * * * * * * * * ANALYSIS OF VARIANCE -- DESIGN 2 * * * * *
TESTS INVOLVING 'MWITHIN B(1) WITHIN C(1), WITHIN-SUBJECT EFFECT

TEST OF SIGNIFICANCE FOR T1 USING UNIQUE SUMS OF SQUARES
SOURCE OF VARIATION            SS        D        MS         F      SIG OF F

WITHIN CELLS                 12.67       6       2.11
MWITHIN B(1) WITHIN          87.11       1      87.11      41.26      .001
C(1)
A BY MWITHIN B(1) WI          8.22       2       4.11       1.95      .223
THIN C(1)
```

FIG. 4.23. Simple simple effect test of the between subjects factor A within the first levels of both repeated measures factors B and C, in a three factor mixed design.

```
* * * * * * * * * * ANALYSIS OF VARIANCE -- DESIGN 2 * * * * *
TESTS INVOLVING 'MWITHIN C(1)' WITHIN-SUBJECT EFFECT

TESTS OF SIGNIFICANCE FOR T1 USING UNIQUE SUMS OF SQUARES
SOURCE OF VARIATION            SS        D        MS         F      SIG OF F

WITHIN CELLS                 11.75      12        .98
MWITHIN C(1)                248.06       1     248.06     253.34      .000
B WITHIN A(1) BY MWI          2.00       1       2.00       2.04      .178
THIN C(1)
B WITHIN A(2) BY MWI          6.12       1       6.12       6.26      .028
THIN C(1)
```

FIG. 4.24. Simple simple effects tests of the between subjects factor B, restricted to the first level of repeated measures factor C, within both the first and second levels of between subjects factor A, in a three factor mixed design.

lines contain both a factor name and a different factor level. The line headings are self-explanatory as to just which simple effect is being tested, and at which level of which other variable the test takes place.

For simple simple effects the line headings are long. For example, a line heading could be A BY MWITHIN B(1) WITHIN C(1), which is the simple simple effect of factor A restricted to the first levels of both repeated measures factors B and C. This heading is sufficiently long to require that it be continued on a second line, with the break sometimes occurring in the middle of a word. Fig. 4.23 offers an illustration of a simple simple effects test of between subjects factor A in a three factor design with two repeated measures factors B and C. Note that, in Fig. 4.23, there is a line heading that only contains levels of factors, and does not contain the name of a different factor. This line is therefore not a meaningful line within the context of this design. There will be separate tables in the printout for the simple simple effects of between subjects factor A at different combined levels of repeated measures factors B and C.

Figure 4.24 offers an illustration of a simple simple effects test of between subjects factor B in a three factor design with one repeated measures factor, C, at both the first and second levels of factor A, restricted to the first level of factor C. In Fig. 4.24 a line to be ignored is the one headed MWITHIN C(1).

5 Multiple Comparisons with a Single Between Subjects Factor

SPSS has a number of tests for multiple comparisons with one factor completely randomized designs. In this chapter the options are examined for a one way analysis of variance with a between subjects factor.

THE TUKEY AND LSD PROCEDURES

Two useful multiple comparison techniques that are available on SPSS, when doing a one way analysis of variance, are the Tukey HSD (honestly significant difference) procedure, which we will call the Tukey test, and the LSD (least significant difference) test. The latter is simply a convenient form of the t test. Both of these are repetitive tests of differences between pairs of means. For example, if there were four groups, there would be six possible tests, each involving one pair of means ($\overline{X}_{.1} - \overline{X}_{.2}, \overline{X}_{.1} - \overline{X}_{.3}, \ldots \overline{X}_{.3} - \overline{X}_{.4}$). The Tukey test, and the LSD test, are each convenient ways of computing a single value against which all of the possible differences between pairs of means can be compared for statistical significance. Thus with six comparisons to be made, a single value would be computed, to determine which differences between means exceed the single value needed for statistical significance.

The Tukey Procedure

The Tukey is used when the intention is to maintain one "family-wise" or "experiment-wise" Type I (alpha) error level. These two names are used by different authors for the following special kind of alpha (α) level: the probability that, if all comparisons are amongst pairs of means from the same population, one or more of the comparisons will be found statistically significant. This varies with the size of the critical value that is used in the comparisons, a single value being used for all comparisons. This value is adjusted for the number of comparisons that are planned, which follows from the number of means (since the Tukey is used when every possible "pair-wise" comparison is to be made). The common "family-wise" alpha level for the Tukey is .05, and that is what is used in SPSS. The test is called up with the RANGES subcommand, under the ONEWAY command. As an example, assume a completely randomized one factor analysis of variance on a factor A, containing four levels, with a dependent variable that is identified as "score" in the program statements. Figure 5.1 offers an illustration of a request for the Tukey test using this example.

Only statement number 4 in Fig. 5.1 is needed for the Tukey test. Notice that RANGES is a subcommand, as seen by its indentation to the fourth space with a preceding slash. The program, as written, will also give the usual analysis of variance summary table, because of the ONEWAY command, and means and standard deviations because of the STATISTICS = DESCRIPTIVES subcommand and keyword.

The Tukey test requires that the harmonic mean be used, in computing the standard error, when the sample sizes of the different groups are not all equal. SPSS uses the harmonic mean when it is requested with the subcommand HARMONIC. In the case of the Tukey test, the harmonic

```
1.TITLE ONEWAY A/V WITH THE TUKEY TEST
2.DATA LIST LIST/A SCORE
3.ONEWAY SCORE BY A(1,4)
4.   /RANGES = TUKEY
5.   /STATISTICS = DESCRIPTIVES
6.BEGIN DATA
  .
  .
  .
```

FIG. 5.1. A sample program for the Tukey test.

```
1.TITLE ONEWAY A/V WITH THE TUKEY TEST
2.DATA LIST LIST/A SCORE
3.ONEWAY SCORE BY A(1,4)
4.   /RANGES = TUKEY
5.   /HARMONIC = ALL
6.   /STATISTICS = DESCRIPTIVES
7.BEGIN DATA
  .
  .
  .
```

FIG. 5.2. A sample program for the Tukey test, with unequal n.

mean should be computed using all of the group means. This requires the use of the keyword ALL. Figure 5.2 illustrates the added subcommand and keyword which would be needed when the sample sizes are different for the different groups.

The harmonic mean and the arithmetic mean are equal when sample sizes are equal, so there is no harm in always using the HARMONIC subcommand, with the ALL keyword, when computing a Tukey test.

The LSD Procedure

The LSD test does not maintain a single "family-wise" alpha level. It is simply a convenient form of the t test, computing a single value against which each desired paired comparison is tested. This criterion value is the tabled critical value for whatever per-comparison alpha level is desired, times the standard error. This criterion value is compared to each difference between means that is to be tested for statistical significance. Again assume a completely randomized one factor analysis of variance on a factor A, with four levels, with a dependent variable which is identified as "score" in the program statements. Figure 5.3 offers an illustrative program, using this example.

The LSD test does not require the harmonic mean with unequal n. Thus the only necessary statement is the RANGES subcommand, followed by an equals sign, followed by the LSD keyword, as seen in program statement 4. The default alpha level is .05, so there is no need to specify the alpha level if you are using .05. If some other alpha level is desired, it follows LSD in parentheses, for example,

```
/RANGES=LSD (.01) .
```

Normally, the LSD test is not done if every possible paired comparison is to be tested; the TUKEY test is then usually what is used (or the Newman–Keuls, or Duncan multiple range test, also available on SPSS). Assume that there are four groups, so that there are four means, yielding six possible paired comparisons. Assume that there is interest in

```
1.TITLE ONEWAY A/V WITH LSD TEST
2.DATA LIST LIST/A SCORE
3.ONEWAY SCORE BY A(1,4)
4.    /RANGES=LSD
5.    /STATISTICS=DESCRIPTIVES
6.BEGIN DATA
 .
 .
 .
```

FIG. 5.3. A sample program for the LSD test.

only three a priori comparisons (involving, for example, some experimental predictions). Although the SPSS program will compute all six comparisons, three can simply be ignored.

The Newman–Keuls and Duncan multiple range tests were alluded to in the preceding paragraph. They can also be called up with keywords under the RANGES subcommand. Specifically,

    /RANGES = SNK

will result in a Newman–Keuls test (identified as the Student–Newman–Keuls by SPSS); and

    /RANGES = DUNCAN

would result in a running of the Duncan multiple range test. SPSS permits up to ten RANGES subcommands for a simple ONEWAY command.

THE SPSS EQUIVALENT TO THE DUNN TEST

There is another common test that can be used for paired comparisons, the Dunn test. The Dunn procedure is used when the decision has been made to test some selected number of pairs, rather than all of the possible pairs among the means, while at the same time maintaining an overall "family-wise" Type I error probability that does not change with the number of comparisons to be made. Maintaining a constant "family-wise" Type I error probability means changing the criterion value for statistical significance, when the number of comparisons change. Thus, the Dunn is used when the intention is to appropriately increase the critical value in terms of the number of comparisons to be made, so that the probability of one or more false instances of statistical significance is constant (at say .05). This can be compared to the common use of the LSD test. The LSD test, like the Dunn, is used for selective comparisons. However, the LSD is not normally used while attempting to maintain a constant "family-wise" alpha level over different numbers of comparisons, whereas the Dunn is used with a constant "family-wise" alpha.

The Dunn, in regard to maintaining a constant "family-wise" alpha level, is similar to the Tukey test. However, the Tukey criterion for statistical significance is more difficult to meet, since it is based on the assumption of making all possible comparisons. The Dunn is the alternative to the Tukey when the intention is to only test a subset of all possible paired comparisons among means, while maintaining a constant "family-wise" Type I error probability.

The Dunn procedure normally consists of consulting a table devised by Dunn (1961), that offers the critical t values for odd Type I error probabilities (such as a per comparison Type I error probability of .0167 when making three comparisons and holding the overall Type I error probability to .05). That is, the Dunn test simply reduces the per comparison Type I error probability as the number of comparisons are increased, in order to maintain a constant "family-wise" Type I error probability. However, the computer does not need to use the Dunn table, since the computer can compute the critical values for t rather than having to look them up. Thus, if the SPSS program can be accessed, the RANGES = LSD subcommand is used, along with a specification of whatever per comparison Type I error probability will be needed, placed in parentheses, at the end of the subcommand. Figure 5.4 illustrates the way in which the equivalent of a Dunn procedure would be requested.

An explanation is needed for the selection of the specific per-comparison value of (.0167) in Fig. 5.4. A simple approximation to the desired per-comparison Type I error probability (α_{pc}) that would maintain a specified overall Type I error probability (α) is

$$\alpha_{pc} = \frac{\alpha}{c} \tag{1}$$

where c is the number of comparisons being made. A more exact equivalence is

$$\alpha = 1 - (1 - \alpha_{pc})^c. \tag{2}$$

However, Equation (1) has a more useful form. If there were three comparisons to be made, Equation (1) would offer

$$\alpha_{pc} = \frac{.05}{3}$$

$$= .0167.$$

```
1.TITLE ONEWAY A/V WITH EQUIVALENT OF A DUNN TEST
2.DATA LIST LIST/A SCORE
3.ONEWAY SCORE BY A(1,4)
4.    /RANGES=LSD (.0167)
5.    /STATISTICS=DESCRIPTIVES
6.BEGIN DATA
.
.
.
```

FIG. 5.4.   A sample program for the equivalent of a DUNN test.

If four comparisons among paired means had been planned, Equation (1) would have yielded

$$\alpha_{pc} = \frac{.05}{4}$$

$$= .0125,$$

which would be entered as

```
/RANGES=LSD (.0125)
```

Usually, the overall Type I error probability, α, is selected as $\alpha = .05$. For five and six comparisons at the .05 level, the α_{pc} values would be

$$.010 = \frac{.05}{5}$$

and

$$.008 \frac{.05}{6}$$

CONTRASTS

An additional form of multiple comparison is needed when we wish to compare sets of means, rather than comparing individual means with each other. For example, with four groups, we might wish to compare the mean of one group (say the control group) with the average of all of the treatment groups, thus comparing one with three. Or we might wish to compare two groups against one, or two groups (say a pair of chemical therapies) against three other groups (involving psychological therapies). Such comparisons are called contrasts, although pair-wise comparisons are included under this general name.

A contrast consists of the sum of two or more means, each multiplied by a **weight** (a value w_j). In this form, a comparison of two means consists of the sum of two means, one multiplied by a weight of $w_1 = +1$, and the other multiplied by a weight of $w_2 = -1$.
This would be symbolized as

$$\left| \sum_j w_j \bar{X}_{.j} \right|,$$

where, for a pair of means $\bar{X}_{.1}$ and $\bar{X}_{.2}$

$$\left|\sum_j w_j \bar{X}_{.j}\right| = |(+1)\bar{X}_{.1} + (-1)\bar{X}_{.2}|$$
$$= |\bar{X}_{.1} - \bar{X}_{.2}|$$

Note that, usually, it is the absolute values of contrasts that are used. If comparing the average of two means against one, there would be a weight of 2 for the single mean, and weights of -1 for each of the two means being averaged, or, a weight of -2 for the single mean and $+1$ for each of the other two means. The same absolute value would result with both sets of weights. Contrasts are available for the MANOVA program as well as ONEWAY.

For the ONEWAY program, the program format seen in Fig. 5.5 would be appropriate.

The weights can be separated by spaces, as in the example, or by commas. CONTRAST, like RANGES, is a subcommand, so is indented four spaces (placed under the fourth column, that is, the W in ONEWAY). The slash preceding each subcommand is also required, as seen in Fig. 5.4. The computation involves a t test, which uses the weights as coefficients of the means in the numerator, and the sum of the *squared* weights ($\sum_j w_j^2$) in the denominator. Specifically, it is

$$t - \frac{\sum_j w_j \bar{X}_{.j}}{\sqrt{\dfrac{MS_w}{n} \sum_j w_j^2}}. \tag{3}$$

The probability value for each t value computed with Equation (3) is given in the printout. There could be some a priori hypotheses about a few particular contrasts that should be tested in this manner. Usually, when testing an a priori hypothesis, any probability value that is less than or

```
1.TITLE ONE FACTOR A/V WITH CONTRASTS
2.DATA LIST LIST/A SCORE
3.ONEWAY SCORE BY A(1,4)
4.    /CONTRAST = -3 1 1 1
5.    /CONTRAST = 0 -2 1 1
6.    /CONTRAST = 0 0 -1 1
7.    /STATISTICS=DESCRIPTIVES
8.BEGIN DATA
.
.
.
```

FIG. 5.5. One factor A/V with contrasts. The space between CONTRAST and the equals sign is not necessary, but is included for visual clarity.

equal to .05 (or .01 in some applications) would indicate statistical significance for the particular contrast. Whenever it is desirable to test several contrasts while maintaining some overall probability level, Equation (1) could be used to determine what the α_{pc} would be, and then this smaller per-comparison alpha value would be used rather than .05 (or .01), as the basis for choosing a critical value for each contrast. The printout would give the probability for each contrast, and those contrasts with probabilities less than or equal to the per comparison alpha level computed with Equation (1) would be considered to be statistically significant.

Up to ten CONTRAST requests can follow any single ONEWAY command. It is possible to use both RANGES and CONTRAST subcommands following the same ONEWAY command (as many as ten of each). It is merely necessary to have the RANGES subcommands placed consecutively.

THE SCHEFFÉ TEST

The previous section discussed complex contrasts among several means, simply done as individual t tests. There is a related multiple comparison test, that, like the Tukey and the Dunn for "pair-wise" comparisons, maintains a constant "family-wise" alpha level when the many comparisons include complex as well as "pair-wise" comparisons. This is the Scheffé procedure.

The Scheffé procedure is an exhaustive search for where the sources of a statistically significant omnibus F might be found. This distinction between the Scheffé and a test of selected a priori contrasts is important, because the researcher pays a high price for using the Scheffé with its very high criterion for statistical significance. Only the strongest effects are detectable with the Scheffé (although there will always be at least one significant Scheffé comparison, given a statistically significant omnibus F test).

Although the Scheffé test can be accessed in SPSS, within SPSS it can only be used for paired comparisons. For this purpose the Tukey test is superior. However, the CONTRAST subcommand can be used to get the basic values needed to compute the Scheffé formula, and therefore permit the use of the Scheffé for more complex comparisons. The most practical form of the formula for the Scheffé procedure, within SPSS, is seen in Equation (4).

$$\left| \sum_j \bar{X}_{\cdot j} \right| \overset{?}{\geq} \sqrt{(a-1)F} \times \sqrt{\frac{MS_w}{n} \sum_j w_j^2} \tag{4}$$

The left hand side of Equation (4) is simply the contrast itself (the weighted difference between means). The right hand side is the critical F value for the omnibus F test, times the number of levels of the factor $(a - 1)$, under the radical. This is multiplied times the standard error, the second component on the right hand side. The standard error contains a sum of the weights squared, so will vary for those sets of contrasts with different weights. This means that different sets of contrasts will have different criterion values for statistical significance.

Scheffé recommended the use of the critical F value for the .10 level of his test, even when the omnibus F test was made at the .05 level. You will have to compute $\sqrt{(a - 1)F}$ by hand, after looking up the F value in an F table. As previously indicated, the program limits you to ten contrasts. Each contrast should individually sum to zero, although the different contrasts do not have to be orthogonal.

To do a Scheffé test for complex contrasts within the SPSS program, you would use the CONTRAST subcommand, which would yield a weighted difference between means. For example, assume that the set of numbers in Table 5.1 constitutes the data from an experiment, which has been analyzed as a completely randomized design. The table also includes the omnibus F test.

Table 5.2 offers eight contrasts, and Fig. 5.6 offers a program in which the eight contrasts of Table 5.2 would be tested, along with the omnibus F test. Within the printout, the contrasts appear in the order in which they

TABLE 5.1
Hypothetical Data from a One Factor Completely Randomized Design, with the Summary Table for the Omnibus F Test

	A_1	A_2	A_3	A_4	A_5
	30	44	54	42	60
	32	32	50	45	54
	40	41	48	55	49
	48	48	47	47	50
	40	50	57	50	50
	44	31	44	49	67
$\overline{X}_{.j} =$	39	41	50	48	35

SV	SS	DF	MS	F
A	1,039.20	4	259.80	6.32
ERROR	1,028.00	25	41.12	
TOT	2,067.20	29		

TABLE 5.2
Eight Contrasts for the Data in Table 1

Contrasts	Groups	Versus	Groups
1.	1&2		3
2.			4
3.			5
4.	1,2,&3		4
5.			5
6.	1,2,&3		4&5
7.	1,2,3,&4		5
8.	1&2		3&4

Adjacent groups on the same line are combined in the contrast. Thus, the first contrast is groups 1 and 2 combined, in a contrast with group 3, and the second and third contrasts are groups one and two combined again, first in a contrast with group 4, and then in a contrast with group 5. The fourth contrast has groups 1, 2, and 3 combined in a contrast with group 4. The last (eighth) contrast in the table is groups 1 and 2 combined in a contrast with groups 3 and 4 combined.

```
TITLE ONE FACTOR COMPLETELY RANDOMIZED DESIGN, EIGHT CONTRASTS
DATA LIST LIST/A SCORE
ONEWAY SCORE BY A(1,5)
  /CONTRAST = -1 -1 2 0 0
  /CONTRAST = -1 -1 0 2 0
  /CONTRAST = -1 -1 0 0 2
  /CONTRAST = -1 -1 -1 3 0
  /CONTRAST = -1 -1 -1 0 3
  /CONTRAST = -2 -2 -2 3 3
  /CONTRAST = -1 -1 -1 -1 4
  /CONTRAST = -1 -1 1 1 0
  /STATISTICS=DESCRIPTIVES
BEGIN DATA
  .
  .
  .
```

FIG. 5.6. Program for the omnibus F test of the data in Table 5.1, along with the CONTRASTS indicated in Table 5.2.

were requested, with the absolute values of the contrasts listed under the heading VALUE, adjacent to the standard error, headed S. ERROR, as seen in Fig. 5.7.

To use Equation (4) to do the Scheffé test, find the section in the printout that looks like Fig. 5.7, and then simply multiply each of the standard

	VALUE	S.ERROR
CONTRAST 1	20.000	6.4124
CONTRAST 2	16.000	6.4125
CONTRAST 3	30.000	6.4125
CONTRAST 4	14.000	9.0686
CONTRAST 5	35.000	9.0686
CONTRAST 6	49.000	14.3388
CONTRAST 7	42.000	11.7075
CONTRAST 8	18.000	5.2358

FIG. 5.7. The computed values of the CONTRASTS of Table 5.2 and Figure 5.6 are found in the printout under the column headed VALUE, adjacent to the standard errors, as seen in this figure. The standard error (S.ERROR), is computed with

$$\sqrt{\frac{MS_w}{n} \sum_i w_i^2}.$$

	VALUE	S.ERROR	CRITERION VALUE	
CONTRAST 1	20.0000*	6.4125	18.936	
CONTRAST 2	16.0000	6.4125	18.936	
CONTRAST 3	30.0000*	6.4125	18.936	
CONTRAST 4	14.0000	9.0686	26.780	$\sqrt{(a-1)F} = 2.953$
CONTRAST 5	35.0000*	9.0686	26.780	
CONTRAST 6	49.0000*	14.3388	42.342	
CONTRAST 7	42.0000*	11.7075	34.572	
CONTRAST 8	18.0000*	5.2358	15.461	

FIG. 5.8. Fig. 5.7, with equation (4) used to compute the criterion values. Asterisks signify statistical significance for individual contrasts. The criterion values are the standard errors times 2.953.

errors times $\sqrt{(a-1)F}$. The products then offer the criterion values for each of the contrasts in the first column. If the contrast exceeds the criterion, the contrast is statistically significant.

In the example discussed in this section (see Table 5.1), the degrees of freedom for looking up the F value, are 4 and 25. Using the recommended .10 level, the tabled critical F value would be found to be 2.18. The value that has to be multiplied times the standard errors would thus be

$$\sqrt{(a-1)F} = \sqrt{(5-1)2.18}$$
$$= \sqrt{8.720}$$
$$= 2.953.$$

Figure 5.8 illustrates what the results of the suggested hand calculations would look like. The last column in Fig. 5.8 offers the results of multiplying $\sqrt{(a-1)F}$ times the standard errors, which in turn are the criterion values for the contrasts. The asterisks indicate which contrasts are statistically significant (because they exceeded the criterion value).

In summary, although the program does not automatically do the full

Scheffé test, it does compute the standard error for each contrast, as well as the empirical values of the contrasts. Thus the program makes it easy to do the full Scheffé test with just a little bit of hand calculation.

THE PRINTOUTS FOR MULTIPLE COMPARISONS

The numbers used in the following examples are taken from Table 5.1. The printout will have a section titled MULTIPLE RANGE TEST for each RANGE subcommand. There are some format variations in this section, the format differing with the use or nonuse of the HARMONIC subcommand. For the Tukey test, with the HARMONIC subcommand, it would look like the material in Fig. 5.9. There is additional material in that section, which will be explained later. The repeated number in Fig. 5.9 (4.15) is the tabled critical value that you would normally find in the appropriate table for the Tukey test. The computer computes it for you, and refers to it later as THE LISTED RANGE. The statement referring to THE ACTUAL RANGE is a reference to the criterion value that has to be reached or exceeded, for any difference between means to be statistically significant. This criterion value is a product of THE LISTED RANGE (the tabled critical value) and the square root of the average within group variance divided by n, the latter being

$$\sqrt{\frac{MS_w}{n}},$$

which in this example is

$$\sqrt{(41.12)/6} = 2.6179.$$

```
MULTIPLE RANGE TEST

TUKEY—HSD PROCEDURE
RANGES FOR THE .05 LEVEL —

        4.15     4.15      4.15

HARMONIC MEAN CELL SIZE = 6.0000

THE ACTUAL RANGE USED IS THE LISTED RANGE * 2.6179
    .
    .
    .
```

FIG. 5.9. Upper section of a large table in the printout material for the Tukey test with the HARMONIC subcommand.

```
                        G G G G G
                        r r r r r
                        p p p p p
   Mean        Group    1 2 4 3 5

  39.0000      Grp 1
  41.0000      Grp 2
  48.0000      Grp 4
  50.0000      Grp 3     *
  55.0000      Grp 5     * *
```

FIG. 5.10. Table of significant differences in a Tukey test.

Thus in the phrase

THE ACTUAL RANGE USED IS THE LISTED RANGE * 2.6179

the asterisk implies multiplication. In the example this would be

$$\text{THE LISTED RANGE} \ * \ \sqrt{\frac{MS_w}{n}} = 4.15 \ \times \ \sqrt{(41.12)/6}$$
$$= 4.15 \ \times \ 2.6179$$
$$= 10.86.$$

This yields the value against which each pair of means is to be compared. A table appears beneath the ACTUAL RANGE that indicates which differences are significant. This table rearranges the means in rank order, and lists the means in a single column, identifying each by its group number (as identified from left to right in the tabled data). A horizontal listing of the same groups, in the same order, is also presented, to form an implied matrix. Any significant differences are noted with an asterisk, as seen in Fig. 5.10, which follows the material seen in Fig. 5.9 within the same large table.

Finally, a statement is offered summarizing which groups have not been found significantly different than each other. Such subsets of groups are given the label of HOMOGENEOUS SUBSETS in the printout. In this example, three homogeneous subsets would be identified, as seen in Fig. 5.11. The HOMOGENEOUS SUBSETS are found at the bottom of the large table which incorporates the material in Figs. 5.9–5.11.

If the sample sizes are equal in the different groups it is not necessary to use the HARMONIC subcommand. If it is not used, the printout will look a little different, although the results will not be changed.

For the LSD procedure, the HARMONIC subcommand should not be used with unequal ns. The printout is a bit more complicated without that subcommand. The part of the table that will be different is reproduced here as Fig. 5.12.

```
SUBSET 1

GROUP      Grp 1     Grp 2      Grp 4
MEAN       39.0000   41.0000    48.0000
- - - - - - - - - - - - - - - - - - - - - - - -


SUBSET 2

GROUP      Grp 2     Grp 4      Grp 3
MEAN       41.0000   48.0000    50.0000
- - - - - - - - - - - - - - - - - - - - - - - -


SUBSET 3

GROUP      Grp 4     Grp 3      Grp 5
MEAN       48.0000   50.0000    55.0000
- - - - - - - - - - - - - - - - - - - - - - - -
```

FIG. 5.11.   Homogeneous subsets identified with the Tukey test.

```
LSD PROCEDURE

RANGES FOR THE 0.050 LEVEL -

          2.91    2.91     2.91      2.91

THE RANGES ABOVE ARE TABLE RANGES

THE VALUE ACTUALLY COMPARED WITH MEANS(J)-MEAN(I) IS..
    4.5343 * RANGE * DSQRT(1/N(I) + 1/N(J))
```

FIG. 5.12.   Part of printout for the LSD test.

The repeated value, 2.91, is identified as RANGE, and it consists of the tabled critical value of t, multiplied by the square root of 2. The criterion value is a function of three values, the RANGE, the square root of the sum of the inverses of the respective sample sizes in the two groups being compared, identified here as DSQRT(1/N(I) + 1/N(J)), and the square root of the within group mean square divided by 2 (which cancels the square root multiplied times the tabled critical value). The resulting formula is equivalent to

$$t \sqrt{2} \sqrt{\frac{MS_w}{2}(1/n_i + 1/n_j)} = t \sqrt{MS_w(1/n_i + 1/n_j)}$$

where t is the tabled critical value and the rest is equivalent to a pooled error term. This then is the criterion value against which the empirical differences are compared. The remainder of the printout material for the LSD test is just like the printout for the Tukey, and does not vary with the use or nonuse of the HARMONIC subcommand.

REFERENCE

Dunn, O. J. (1961). Multiple comparisons among means. *Journal of the American Statistical Association, 56*, 52–64.

6 Contrasts with Repeated Measures and Multiple Factors

In SPSS, specific tests for multiple comparisons, such as the Tukey test or Least Significant Difference (LSD) test, are not possible with repeated measures, or with multiple factors. However, the CONTRAST and TRANSFORM subcommands under the MANOVA command can be used for multiple comparisons. CONTRAST under MANOVA is different than CONTRAST under ONEWAY, so the procedures found in this chapter under the CONTRAST subcommand are different than those described in the preceding chapter under ONEWAY.

COMPLETELY RANDOMIZED DESIGNS

This section begins with the use of MANOVA for a multifactor completely randomized design, to request tests of a set of contrasts, as expressed in Fig. 6.1.

There are no repeated measures in the design requested in Fig. 6.1, so none are present in either the DATA LIST or MANOVA command lines. This makes it possible to omit the WSFACTORS subcommand. A special CONTRAST subcommand is used, with the factor concerned in parentheses, followed by an equals sign. The desired contrasts, that is, the weights in the contrast, are indicated within parentheses, following the equals sign and the keyword SPECIAL. The contrasts must be equivalent

```
TITLE TWO FACTORS, COMPLETELY RANDOMIZED
SUBTITLE ONE SET OF CONTRASTS ON ONE FACTOR
DATA LIST LIST/A B SCORE
MANOVA SCORE BY A(1,3) B(1,3)
   /CONTRAST(A)=SPECIAL(3*1, 1,0,-1, -1,2,-1)
   /PRINT=CELLINFO(MEANS)
   /DESIGN=A(1) A(2)
BEGIN DATA
   .
   .
   .
```

FIG. 6.1. Test of one set of contrasts, on one factor, in a two factor completely randomized design.

to a square matrix, where there are as many contrasts as there are levels of the factor. For example,

```
/CONTRAST(A)=SPECIAL(   1, 1, 1,
                        1, 0,-1,
                       -1, 2,-1 )
```

The first contrast in the set of contrasts following a CONTRAST subcommand is required for the program, and merely consists of a series of ones. The other contrasts will be the contrasts of interest. The weights can also be placed consecutively, as seen in the sample program in Fig. 6.1. There it can be seen that, rather than simply repeating the ones, the number of ones (here 3), can be specified, and then followed by an asterisk to mean "times," and then a one,

```
(3*1, 1,0,-1, -1,2,-1)
```

When the weights for the different contrasts are placed in a set consecutively on a line, the contrasts are clearer if each contrast in a set of contrasts is followed by a comma and a space, with the numbers within a contrast separated by a comma with no space. (The program accepts either a comma or a space as a means of distinguishing the weights.)

Each contrast (other than the set of ones) should be labeled in the DESIGN subcommand, using the name for the factor (here A), followed by a number in parentheses, the first A followed by a (1), the second by a (2), etc., that is,

```
DESIGN=A(1) A(2)
```

In Fig. 6.1 factor A has two contrasts needing labels, so they receive the labels A(1) and A(2) in the DESIGN subcommand. These labels will serve to identify the tests of the individual contrasts in the printout. In summary, for a between subjects factor in a multifactor design, specifications are added to two subcommands: CONTRAST, and DESIGN.

If the decision is made to examine contrasts on both factors, the CONTRAST subcommand is repeated in the position within the program shown in Fig. 6.2. Note the labeling of both sets of contrasts in the DESIGN subcommand.

Within any one contrast request the set of contrast weights should be orthogonal, as is the case in Fig. 6.1. If a needed contrast destroys the orthogonality, replace it and request the needed contrast in a separate CONTRAST subcommand. You have to add this request to the end of the program following the last DESIGN subcommand. That is, a requirement for additional contrasts on the same factor is that the request has to follow a DESIGN subcommand, and have its own DESIGN subcommand. It therefore involves a second sequential use of the CONTRAST and DESIGN subcommands, as seen in Fig. 6.3.

The labels for the contrasts have to include the numbers 1, 2, etc., as in A(1), A(2), when the contrasts involve between subjects factors. Thus you could not label the second set of contrasts differently, as, for example,

```
TITLE TWO FACTORS, COMPLETELY RANDOMIZED
SUBTITLE CONTRASTS ON BOTH FACTORS
DATA LIST LIST/A B SCORE
MANOVA SCORE BY A(1,3) B(1,3)
  /CONTRAST(A)=SPECIAL(3*1, 1,0,-1, -1,2,-1)
  /CONTRAST(B)=SPECIAL(3*1, 2,-1,-1, 0,1,-1)
  /PRINT=CELLINFO(MEANS)
  /DESIGN=A(1) A(2) B(1) B(2)
BEGIN DATA
     .
     .
     .
```

FIG. 6.2. Contrasts on both factors, in a completely randomized two factor design.

```
TITLE TWO FACTORS, COMPLETELY RANDOMIZED
SUBTITLE TWO SEPARATE SETS OF CONTRASTS ON THE SAME FACTOR
DATA LIST LIST/A B SCORE
MANOVA SCORE BY A(1,3) B(1,3)
  /CONTRAST(A)=SPECIAL(3*1, 1,0,-1, -1,2,-1)
  /PRINT=CELLINFO(MEANS)
  /DESIGN=A(1) A(2)
  /CONTRAST(A)=SPECIAL(3*1, 2,-1,-1, 0,1,-1)
  /DESIGN=A(1) A(2)
BEGIN DATA
     .
     .
     .
```

FIG. 6.3. Two separate tests of contrasts, on the same factor, in a two factor completely randomized design.

A(3) A(4). In order to identify which contrast is which in the printout, you have to keep track of which contrasts occur first in the program; those that occur first in the program will appear first in the printout.

If you wish to include the omnibus and interaction F tests along with the tests of contrasts, you simply include a DESIGN subcommand with nothing else on that line (no equal sign or anything following on that line), at the end of the program. This is seen in Fig. 6.4.

Interaction of Contrasts with Between Subjects Factors

When there is more than one between subjects factor, there can be interest in the interaction of the contrasts. A context for this question is seen in Fig. 6.4, in which there are two between subjects factors A and B, each with three levels, and contrast requests on both factors, as expressed in the following three subcommands taken from Fig. 6.4.

```
/CONTRAST(A)=SPECIAL(3*1, 2,-1,-1, 0,1,-1)
/CONTRAST(B)=SPECIAL(3*1, 1,0,-1, -1,2,-1)
/DESIGN=A(1) A(2) B(1) B(2)
```

To have the printout include a test of the interaction of say the first contrast of A, with factor B, the design subcommand should include the specification A(1) BY B within the DESIGN subcommand, looking like the following:

```
/DESIGN=A(1) A(2) B(1) B(2) A(1) BY B
```

This specification would ask the question of whether the contrast $2, -1, -1$ (which is a comparison of the first level of A with the average of the other two levels of A), yielded different results at the different levels of B. A similar but more specific question would be posed by the interaction A(1) BY B(1). This would be a question of the interaction of the contrasts

```
TITLE TWO FACTORS, COMPLETELY RANDOMIZED, FULL ANALYSIS
SUBTITLE PLUS CONTRASTS ON BOTH FACTORS
DATA LIST LIST/A B SCORE
MANOVA SCORE BY A(1,3) B(1,3)
  /CONTRAST(A)=SPECIAL(3*1, 2,-1,-1, 0,1,-1)
  /CONTRAST(B)=SPECIAL(3*1, 1,0,-1, -1,2,-1)
  /PRINT=CELLINFO(MEANS)
  /DESIGN=A(1) A(2) B(1) B(2)
  /DESIGN
BEGIN DATA
  .
  .
  .
```

FIG. 6.4. Contrasts on both factors, in a completely randomized two factor design, with a request for the omnibus and interaction F tests.

$2, -1, -1$ of A with the contrast $1, 0, -1$ of B. The specific meaning of this contrast, is whether the A contrast $2, -1, -1$, would yield different results at the first versus the third level of B $(1, 0, -1)$.

The number of degrees of freedom for the interaction limits the number of interaction contrasts that can be included in the DESIGN subcommand. For example, the general interaction A BY B, with three levels of both factors, has four degrees of freedom. One could ask, therefore, for some subset of interactions which at most add up to four degrees of freedom. As an example, A(1) BY B, and A(2) BY B each have two degrees of freedom, so both of these could be requested in the DESIGN subcommand. Another alternative, would be to ask for up to four different single degree of freedom tests in the example: A(1) BY B(1) A(1) BY B(2) A(2) BY B(1) A(2) BY B(2). These requests would simply follow on the DESIGN subcommand after A(1) (A2) B(1) B(2). An example of interaction requests is seen in Fig. 6.5.

```
TITLE TWO FACTORS, COMPLETELY RANDOMIZED, FULL ANALYSIS
SUBTITLE PLUS CONTRASTS ON BOTH FACTORS AND CONTRAST INTERACTION
DATA LIST LIST/A B SCORE
MANOVA SCORE BY A(1,3) B(1,3)
  /CONTRAST(A)=SPECIAL(3*1, 1,0,-1,  -1,2,-1)
  /CONTRAST(B)=SPECIAL(3*1, 2,-1,-1,  0,1,-1)
  /PRINT=CELLINFO(MEANS)
  /DESIGN=A(1) A(2) B(1) B(2) A(1) BY B A(2) BY B(1)
  /DESIGN
BEGIN DATA
  .
  .
  .
```

FIG. 6.5. Contrasts on both factors, in a completely randomized two factor design, along with a test of an interaction of one contrast of A with Factor B, and interaction of the other contrast of A with one of the contrasts of B. A request for the omnibus and interaction F tests is also included, via the final DESIGN subcommand.

REPEATED MEASURES DESIGNS

In this section orthogonal sets of contrasts are assumed. If the set of requested contrasts on one factor is nonorthogonal, use of the CONTRAST subcommand will result in the contrasts being transformed so as to be orthogonal, affecting the outcomes of the tests. For sets of nonorthogonal contrasts with repeated measures, the TRANSFORM subcommand should be used. The TRANSFORM subcommand is discussed in the immediately following section. With orthogonal sets of contrasts either the CONTRAST or TRANSFORM subcommands can be used. It is generally more convenient to the running of the rest of the program to use the CONTRAST subcommand. Use of the CONTRAST subcommand with a repeated measures factor is illustrated in Fig. 6.6, which offers a program for a one factor repeated measures design with a request for a set of contrasts.

Note that in Fig. 6.6 the RENAME subcommand is included. This is an optional subcommand. Including it merely adds to the clarity in reading the printouts. If the RENAME subcommand is included, it must contain as many names as there are levels for the factor being tested for contrasts. The factor in the program in Fig. 6.6 has three levels, so there must be three names following an equals sign within the RENAME subcommand. The names chosen can be any labels that will be informative to the reader of the printout, since they will appear next to the tests for the contrasts within the printout. (No more than eight letters and/or numbers can be used per name, although a name cannot begin with a number.) The first name will be applied to the set of ones, and so a name such as CONSTANT or MEAN might be appropriate. But the remaining names can usefully be called FIRST, SECOND, etc., so that the printout will label the tests of each of these contrasts as the first, second, etc. No specifications are added to the DESIGN subcommand when a repeated measure is being tested for contrasts.

There is one more change required for contrasts on repeated measures. When testing contrasts with repeated measures, a second specification, SIGNIF(UNIV), should be added to the PRINT subcommand, so that the subcommand will look like

```
/PRINT = CELLINFO(MEANS) SIGNIF(UNIV)
```

This addition of SIGNIF(UNIV) will instruct the program to include some necessary univariate tests in the printout.

In summary, for contrasts on a repeated measure, the WSFACTORS subcommand should be present. The PRINT subcommand has an added specification, and the DESIGN subcommand loses its specifications. As an option, the RENAME subcommand can be used to supply labels for the tests of contrasts on a repeated measure.

```
TITLE ONE FACTOR REPEATED MEASURES DESIGN
SUBTITLE ONE SET OF CONTRASTS
DATA LIST LIST/C1 C2 C3
MANOVA C1 C2 C3
   /WSFACTORS = C(3)
   /CONTRAST(C) = SPECIAL(3*1, 2, -1, -1, 0, 1, -1)
   /RENAME = MEAN FIRST SECOND
   /PRINT = CELLINFO(MEANS) SIGNIF(UNIV)
   /DESIGN
BEGIN DATA
   .
   .
   .
```

FIG. 6.6. Test of one set of contrasts on a repeated measures factor, in a one factor repeated measures design. This program will also yield an omnibus F test and other related information.

```
TITLE ONE FACTOR REPEATED MEASURES DESIGN
SUBTITLE TWO SETS OF CONTRASTS
DATA LIST LIST/C1 C2 C3
MANOVA C1 C2 C3
   /WSFACTORS = C(3)
   /CONTRAST(C) = SPECIAL(3*1, 2, -1, -1, 0, 1, -1)
   /RENAME = MEAN FIRST SECOND
   /PRINT = CELLINFO(MEANS) SIGNIF(UNIV)
   /DESIGN
   /CONTRAST(C) = SPECIAL(3*1, -1, 0, 1, 1, -2, 1)
   /DESIGN
BEGIN DATA
   .
   . .
   .
```

FIG. 6.7.   Test of two sets of contrasts in a one factor repeated measures design.

If you wish to do additional contrasts on the same factor, you add this request to the end of the program, following the DESIGN subcommand, as seen in Fig. 6.7.

Only one RENAME subcommand has been used in the program in Fig. 6.7, since the same labels can be used for both sets of contrasts. The first set will appear in the printout under the DESIGN 1 heading, and the second under the DESIGN 2 heading. That is, the printout headings indicate which DESIGN subcommand followed the request.

Note that, in Fig. 6.7, the two sets of contrasts on the same factor mean four different contrasts, when only two orthogonal simultaneous contrasts can be orthogonal (given a three level factor). The program will give you correct contrasts that are not orthogonal, when the nonorthogonal contrasts are requested in different CONTRAST subcommands, and each CONTRAST subcommand precedes its own DESIGN subcommand.

Requesting Nonorthogonal Contrasts with the Transform Subcommand

The TRANSFORM subcommand can be used in place of the CONTRAST subcommand, in order to obtain nonorthogonal sets of contrasts with repeated measures. The TRANSFORM subcommand is used with the same keywords as the CONTRAST subcommand, although the levels of the variable are placed in parentheses, where the CONTRAST subcommand would have the name of the factor. As an example, assume a request for a set of nonorthogonal contrasts on a repeated measures factor C, with four levels, C1, C2, C3, and C4. In place of the CONTRAST subcommand, one could use

```
/TRANSFORM(C1 C2 C3 C4) = SPECIAL(4*1, 1, 0, 0, -1, 1, 1, 0, -2,
   1, 1, 1, -3)
```

because the contrasts are not orthogonal. If the contrasts were orthogonal, the subcommand CONTRAST would be used in place of TRANSFORM, still using SPECIAL as a keyword, but following it with (C) rather than (C1 C2 C3 C4). Figure 6.8 illustrates the use of the TRANSFORM subcommand.

An important difference in the use of the TRANSFORM subcommand, is that the WSFACTORS subcommand must be omitted (as illustrated in Fig. 6.8). This in turn means that the regular analysis, the omnibus F test, would not be done, only the contrasts would be computed. To obtain the omnibus F test on the factor (C in this example), request the omnibus F test first, with the WSFACTORS subcommand, and then, after the END DATA command, add a second MANOVA command, followed by the TRANSFORM subcommand, as seen in Fig. 6.9.

```
TITLE ONE FACTOR REPEATED MEASURES DESIGN
SUBTITLE ONE SET OF NON-ORTHOGONAL CONTRASTS
DATA LIST LIST/C1 C2 C3 C3
MANOVA C1 C2 C3 C4
  /TRANSFORM(C1 C2 C3 C4)=SPECIAL(4*1, 1,0,0,-1, 1,1,0,-2,
    1,1,1,-3)
  /RENAME=MEAN FIRST SECOND THIRD
  /PRINT=CELLINFO(MEANS)
  /DESIGN
BEGIN DATA
  .
  .
  .
```

FIG. 6.8. Use of the TRANSFORM subcommand to obtain nonorthogonal contrasts with a single repeated measure.

```
TITLE ONE FACTOR REPEATED MEASURES DESIGN
SUBTITLE ONE SET OF NON-ORTHOGONAL CONTRASTS PLUS OMNIBUS F
DATA LIST LIST/C1 C2 C3 C3
MANOVA C1 C2 C3 C4
  /WSFACTORS=C(4)
  /PRINT=CELLINFO(MEANS)
  /DESIGN
BEGIN DATA
  .
  .
  .
END DATA
MANOVA C1 C2 C3 C4
  /TRANSFORM(C1 C2 C3 C4)=SPECIAL(4*1, 1,0,0,-1, 1,1,0,-2,
    1,1,1,-3)
  /RENAME=MEAN FIRST SECOND THIRD
  /NOPRINT=SIGNIF(UNIV MULTIV)
  /DESIGN
```

FIG. 6.9. Example of the use of the TRANSFORM subcommand to obtain nonorthogonal contrasts, while at the same time obtaining the omnibus F test.

The use of two MANOVA commands could lead to some repetition in the printout. The NOPRINT subcommand, as seen in Fig. 6.9, tells the printout which material to omit. The keyword SIGNIF and the further specifications UNIV AND MULTIV, stop the printout from repeating the significance tests that have appeared in the first part of the printout.

Multiple Related Measures and Interactions of Contrasts

If there are two or more repeated measures in a design, the levels of the different repeated measures must all be combined so as to appear as a single repeated measure in the DATA LIST and MANOVA commands. For example, given two repeated measures, B, with two levels, and C, with three levels, the two factors would be combined into six levels, possibly labeled, B1C1 B1C2 B1C3 B2C1 B2C2 B2C3, if the data were entered with factor B changing more slowly, as discussed in chapter Two. Recall that, if the RENAME subcommand is used it requires that there be as many labels as there are levels of the repeated measures factor. With two (or more) repeated measures factors the levels are combined as just described, so the RENAME subcommand will have as many labels as levels are produced by combining all of the repeated measures. If there are j levels of one factor, and k levels of the other factor, there will be a total of j times k measurements (combined levels). A concrete example should make the procedure clear. Figure 6.10 offers a program for a test of a set of contrasts on factor C in a two factor repeated measures design.

The RENAME subcommand has six names, because the two factors, one with two and the other with three levels, produce two times three equals six levels. The selection of the names used in the RENAME subcommand in Fig. 6.10 is not arbitrary, although the program will accept any names that are entered, as long as they do not include more than eight letters. The first name, as usual, refers to the contrast of ones. The next

```
TITLE TWO REPEATED MEASURES, TESTING ONE (C) FOR CONTRASTS
DATA LIST LIST/B1C1 B1C2 B1C3 B2C1 B2C2 B2C3
MANOVA B1C1 B1C2 B1C3 B2C1 B2C2 B2C3
  /WSFACTORS=B(2) C(3)
  /CONTRAST(C)=SPECIAL(3*1, 2,-1,-1, 0,1,-1)
  /RENAME=MEAN B FIRST SECOND INTER1 INTER2
  /PRINT=CELLINFO(MEANS) SIGNIF(UNIV)
  /DESIGN
BEGIN DATA
  .
  .
  .
```

FIG. 6.10.   Test of a set of contrasts on one of two repeated measures, in a two factor design.

```
TITLE TWO REPEATED MEASURES, TESTING BOTH FOR CONTRASTS
DATA LIST LIST/B1C1 B1C2 B1C3 B2C1 B2C2 B2C3 B3C1
  B3C2 B3C3
MANOVA B1C1 B1C2 B1C3 B2C1 B2C2 B2C3 B3C1 B3C2 B3C3
  /WSFACTORS=B(3) C(3)
  /CONTRAST(C)=SPECIAL(3*1, 2,-1,-1, 0,1,-1)
  /CONTRAST(B)=SPECIAL(3*1, -1,0,1, 1,-2,1)
  /RENAME=MEAN B1 B2 C1 C2 B1XC1 B1XC2 B2XC1 B2XC2
  /PRINT=CELLINFO(MEANS) SIGNIF(UNIV)
  /DESIGN
BEGIN DATA
  .
  .
  .
```

FIG. 6.11.   Contrasts on both factors in a two factor repeated measures design.

one refers to the most slowly changing factor, that is, factor B. The third and fourth names refer to the two contrasts being tested. This arrangement of names is useful because the printout will then have the labels FIRST and SECOND next to the desired contrasts on factor C.

The final two names in the RENAME subcommand in Fig. 6.10 refer to the interactions between the specified contrasts on C and contrasts on B. If no contrasts are specified on the second factor (B in this example), the program imposes its own contrasts. With only two levels on the second factor (B), the imposed contrast is $1, -1$, making the interaction of contrasts equivalent to an interaction of the contrast on factor C with factor B. That is, in Fig. 6.10, INTER1 is the label for the test of whether the first contrast of factor C is different at the two levels of factor B. INTER2 asks the same question about the second contrast of factor C.

Assume, however, that there are more than two levels for the second factor. An example of this is seen in Fig. 6.11. In Fig. 6.11 it is necessary to distinguish the different contrasts, as well as the different interactions of contrasts. The second through fifth names in the RENAME subcommand, B1, B2, C1, and C2, specify the four requested contrasts. The contrasts on the most slowly changing factor are always represented first. The labels B1XC1 B1XC2 B2XC1 B2XC2 specify which interactions of contrasts are being tested. In general, they will follow the order of the most slowly changing factor first, remaining unchanged until interactions with all levels of the other factor have been represented.

The following statement summarizes the order of labels with the RENAME subcommand: The first name refers to the contrast of ones. The next j-1 names refer to the j-1 contrasts on the most slowly changing factor (which has j levels). The next k-1 names refer to the k-1 contrasts on the next most slowly changing factor (which has k levels). If there is a third factor, its position is determined by which factors change before it and after it.

If there were five levels of the most slowly changing factor, and three of another factor, then the first four labels following MEAN would refer to the contrasts on the most slowly changing factor, and the next two to the contrasts on the other factor. The last few labels would refer to interactions of the contrasts. Still assuming five levels of one factor and three of the other, among the five times three equals fifteen labels, there would be four, times two, equals eight, interactions of contrasts represented. In general, given two factors with j and k levels, there will be (j-1)(k-1) interactions tested, so the last (j-1)(k-1) labels will refer to interactions.

As previously indicated, when there is a contrast request on a repeated measure, the PRINT command should include the keywords SIGNIF(UNIV), in order to for the univariate significance tests of the contrasts to appear in the printout. If there are two repeated measures factors in the design, with this request for univariate significance tests in the PRINT subcommand, the program will impose contrasts on any second factor for which contrasts are not requested. The program will then use the imposed contrasts to compute the interactons of contrasts. These interaction tests can be ignored in the printout unless the user is interested in particular contrast interactions. If the interactions are of interest, the user should impose desired weights, and use labels in the RENAME subcommand that will be informative, as suggested in the preceding example.

The order in which the CONTRAST subcommands are given (that is, whether B or C is requested first) is not important. In Fig. 6.11, where the request for contrasts on C preceded the request for contrasts on B, the order of the two CONTRAST subcommands could have been reversed without affecting the program. The order is only crucial within the WSFACTORS subcommand, where the most slowly changing must be first.

Note that, in Fig. 6.11, the two CONTRAST subcommands are adjacent, and share the same DESIGN subcommand. That is permissible as long as the contrast requests are for different repeated measures factors. If a second set of contrasts is requested for the *same* factor, it has to follow the DESIGN subcommand, and be followed by a second DESIGN subcommand, as seen previously in Fig. 6.7.

The Interaction of a Contrast with Another Factor.   In the preceding paragraphs the discussion of contrast interactions primarily concerned the interaction of two sets of contrasts. A different question concerning contrasts, is the question of whether the contrasts on one factor are simply different at the different levels of a second factor; that is, the question could be asked as to whether there is an interaction of a contrast on one factor with the second factor (rather than an interaction of contrasts). For example, assume that, for the program in Fig. 6.11, there was a question of whether there is a significant interaction of the first contrast of B with factor C. To answer this question with two repeated measures factors, the WSDESIGN subcommand must be added to the program, along with some specifications. For the program in Fig. 6.11, the added specification could be the following:

```
/WSDESIGN=B(1) BY C
```

The use of a parenthesized 1 following the name of the contrast factor identifies the first contrast in the set. If the interaction of interest concerned the second contrast, then

```
/WSDESIGN=B(2) BY C
```

would be appropriate.

Recall that this same specification was used in the DESIGN subcommand for between subjects factors. All such specifications for between subjects factors are always made in the DESIGN subcommand, while such specifications for within subjects (repeated measures) factors are made in the WSDESIGN subcommand.

A problem in adding specifications to the WSDESIGN subcommand, is that the *only* within subject analyses that are done are those requested in the WSDESIGN subcommand, unless it is omitted, in which case a full analysis is done. For this reason, the WSDESIGN subcommand with specifications is generally presented after the request for the omnibus F tests, permitting these other tests to also be run. This is done by presenting the WSDESIGN subcommand with no specifications before one DESIGN subcommand, and then again, with specifications, following the DESIGN subcommand. An example is seen in Fig. 6.12, where the second WSDE-

```
TITLE TWO REPEATED MEASURES, TESTING BOTH FOR CONTRASTS
SUBTITLE ADDING AN INTERACTION SPECIFICATION
DATA LIST LIST/B1C1 B1C2 B1C3 B2C1 B2C2 B2C3 B3C1 B3C2 B3C3
MANOVA B1C1 B1C2 B1C3 B2C1 B2C2 B2C3 B3C1 B3C2 B3C3
   /WSFACTORS=B(3) C(3)
   /CONTRAST(B)=SPECIAL(3*1, 2,-1,-1, 0,1,-1)
   /CONTRAST(C)=SPECIAL(3*1, -1,0,1, 1,-2,1)
   /RENAME=MEAN B1 B2 C1 C2 B1XC1 B1XC2 B2XC1 B2XC2
   /PRINT=CELLINFO(MEANS) SIGNIF(UNIV)
   /WSDESIGN
   /DESIGN
   /WSDESIGN=C(1) BY B C(2) BY B
   /DESIGN
BEGIN DATA
   .
   .
   .
```

FIG. 6.12.   Test of contrasts on both of the factors in a two factor repeated measures design. A request for a test of the interaction of each contrast of C with factor B has been added, using the WSDESIGN subcommand.

SIGN subcommand has the specifications C(1) BY B C(2) BY B, which are requests for the interaction of each contrast of C with factor B.

Summary of Trend Interaction Tests Comparing Completely Randomized with Repeated Measures Designs

In summary, the SPSS program treats between and within subjects factors differently in regard to contrast interactions. Given two between subjects factors, and contrast requests for both, all interactions involving contrasts have to be specifically requested on the DESIGN subcommand, or they are not computed. Given two repeated measures factors, and contrast requests for both, the interactions of the requested contrasts will automatically appear in the printout. The only ones that have to be requested (if they are desired) are the interactions of each contrast with another factor; and these have to be requested on the WSDESIGN subcommand, when working with repeated measures.

MIXED DESIGNS

In mixed designs requests for contrasts on repeated measures follow the form seen in the previous section. Examples in the context of mixed designs are offered below.

Contrasts on Repeated Measures Factors in Mixed Designs

Figure 6.13 offers an example of a program for a contrast request on a repeated measure (C) in a two factor mixed design.

```
TITLE TWO FACTORS, ONE REPEATED MEASURE (C)
SUBTITLE CONTRASTS ON THE REPEATED MEASURE
DATA LIST LIST/A C1 C2 C3
MANOVA C1 C2 C3 BY A(1,3)
   /WSFACTORS = C(3)
   /CONTRAST(C) = SPECIAL(3*1, 2, -1, -1, 0,1, -1)
   /RENAME = MEAN C1 C2
   /PRINT = CELLINFO(MEANS) SIGNIF(UNIV)
   /DESIGN
BEGIN DATA
   .
   .
   .
```

FIG. 6.13.   Contrasts on a repeated measure in a two factor mixed design.

The same program would be used for a design in which there were additional between subjects factors, with the placement of the names of the additional between subjects factors in the usual places within the DATA LIST and MANOVA commands. For example, if a between subjects factor B, with four levels, were added to the design, the DATA LIST and MANOVA commands would look like the following:

```
DATA LIST LIST/A B C1 C2 C3
MANOVA C1 C2 C3 BY A(1,3) B(1,4)
```

If instead of a between subjects factor, a repeated measures factor B were added to the program, the DATA LIST and MANOVA commands, as well as the RENAME subcommand, would be lengthened, as seen in Fig. 6.14.

If additional contrasts were desired on the same repeated measure, it would follow the DESIGN subcommand, as previously seen in Fig. 6.7, and illustrated for the mixed design in Fig. 6.15.

```
TITLE THREE FACTORS, TWO REPEATED MEASURES (B & C)
SUBTITLE CONTRASTS ON ONE REPEATED MEASURE (C)
DATA LIST LIST/A B1C1 B1C2 B1C3 B2C1 B2C2 B2C3
MANOVA B1C1 B1C2 B1C3 B2C1 B2C2 B2C3 BY A(1,3)
   /WSFACTORS=B(2) C(3)
   /CONTRAST(C)=SPECIAL(3*1, 2,-1,-1, 0,1,-1)
   /RENAME=MEAN B C1 C2 INTER1 INTER2
   /PRINT=CELLINFO(MEANS) SIGNIF(UNIV)
   /DESIGN
BEGIN DATA
      .
      .
      .
```

FIG. 6.14. Contrasts on one of two repeated measures in a mixed design.

```
TITLE THREE FACTORS, TWO REPEATED MEASURES (B & C)
SUBTITLE TWO CONTRASTS ON ONE REPEATED MEASURE (C)
DATA LIST LIST/A B1C1 B1C2 B1C3 B2C1 B2C2 B2C3
MANOVA B1C1 B1C2 B1C3 B2C1 B2C2 B2C3 BY A(1,3)
   /WSFACTORS=B(2) C(3)
   /CONTRAST(C)=SPECIAL(3*1, 2,-1,-1, 0,1,-1)
   /RENAME=MEAN B C1 C2 INTER1 INTER2
   /PRINT=CELLINFO(MEANS) SIGNIF(UNIV)
   /DESIGN
   /CONTRAST(C)=SPECIAL(3*1, -1,0,1, 1,-2,1)
   /DESIGN
BEGIN DATA
      .
      .
      .
```

FIG. 6.15. Two contrasts on the same repeated measure in a mixed three factor design with two repeated measures.

```
TITLE THREE FACTORS, TWO REPEATED MEASURES (B & C)
SUBTITLE CONTRASTS ON BOTH REPEATED MEASURES
DATA LIST LIST/A B1C1 B1C2 B1C3 B2C1 B2C2 B2C3 B3C1
  B3C2 B3C3
MANOVA B1C1 B1C2 B1C3 B2C1 B2C2 B2C3 B3C1 B3C2 B3C3 BY A(1,3)
  /WSFACTORS=B(3) C(3)
  /CONTRAST(C)=SPECIAL(3*1, 2,-1,-1, 0,1,-1)
  /CONTRAST(B)=SPECIAL(3*1, -1,0,1, 1,-2,1)
  /RENAME=MEAN B1 B2 C1 C2 B1XC1 B1XC2 B2XC1 B2XC2
  /PRINT=CELLINFO(MEANS) SIGNIF(UNIV)
  /DESIGN
BEGIN DATA
  .
  .
  .
```

FIG. 6.16. Contrasts on both repeated measures in a three factor mixed design.

```
TITLE TWO FACTORS, ONE REPEATED MEASURE (C)
SUBTITLE CONTRAST ON THE BETWEEN SUBJECTS FACTOR (A)
DATA LIST LIST/A C1 C2 C3
MANOVA C1 C2 C3 BY A(1,3)
  /WSFACTORS=C(3)
  /PRINT=CELLINFO(MEANS)
  /DESIGN
  /CONTRAST(A)=SPECIAL(3*1, 1,0,-1, -1,2,-1)
  /DESIGN=A(1) A(2)
BEGIN DATA
  .
  .
  .
```

FIG. 6.17. Contrast on a between subjects factor in a two factor mixed design.

If contrasts are desired on two repeated measures in a mixed design, a second CONTRAST subcommand follows the first, as previously seen in Fig. 6.11, and illustrated for the mixed design in Fig. 6.16. Discussion of the features of the program in Fig. 6.16 is found at the end of the preceding section, in connection with the similar program in Fig. 6.11. In that section interaction of contrasts on repeated measures is discussed.

Contrasts on Between Subjects Factors in Mixed Designs

For the test of a contrast of a between subjects factor in a mixed design, the request for the omnibus F tests, or at least simple effects tests, must precede the request for contrasts. This is illustrated in Fig. 6.17, which offers a program for a contrast on the between subjects factor in a two factor mixed design.

Note the absence of SIGNIF(UNIV) in the PRINT subcommand, in Fig. 6.17, because the only contrast is for a between subjects factor. There is really nothing wrong with continuing to use SIGNIF(UNIV) for all contrasts. However, whenever SIGNIF(UNIV) is used there are additional tables produced, which are only useful when there is a contrast requested on a repeated measures factor. Unnecessary use of SIGNIF(UNIV) can lead to some confusion in reading the printouts.

Additional sets of contrasts on the same factor can be requested, but must follow the last DESIGN subcommand. Put another way, each additional request for a set of contrasts on the same factor must be separated by a DESIGN subcommand. This is illustrated in Fig. 6.18.

Note that the same labels must be used for both sets of contrasts. The order of the contrast requests will be maintained in the printout, which simplifies differentiating them. Each set of contrasts appears in a table that indicates, at the very top, which DESIGN subcommand the contrast request has preceded in the program. With additional between subjects factors in the design, the program for contrasts on any one of the between subjects factors will be the same as that seen in Fig. 6.18 (except for specification of the additional factors in the DATA LIST and MANOVA commands).

Contrasts can be done on more than one between subjects factor, as illustrated in Fig. 6.19, where it is indicated that contrasts on different between subjects factors do not have to be separated by a DESIGN subcommand.

Figure 6.20 illustrates the same program as that seen in Fig. 6.19, except that some tests of interactions of contrasts with the other between subjects factor are requested.

The discussion of interactions among between subjects contrasts appears earlier, within the section titled Interaction of Contrasts with Between Subjects Factors.

```
TITLE TWO FACTORS, ONE REPEATED MEASURE (C)
SUBTITLE TWO CONTRASTS ON FACTOR A
DATA LIST LIST/A C1 C2 C3
MANOVA C1 C2 C3 BY A(1,3)
   /WSFACTORS = C(3)
   /PRINT = CELLINFO(MEANS)
   /DESIGN
   /CONTRAST(A) = SPECIAL(3*1, 1,0,-1,  -1,2,-1)
   /DESIGN = A(1) A(2)
   /CONTRAST(A) = SPECIAL(3*1, 2,-1,-1,  0,1,-1)
   /DESIGN = A(1) A(2)
BEGIN DATA
   .
   .
   .
```

FIG. 6.18.   Two contrasts on the same between subjects factor in a two factor mixed design.

Contrasts on both Between and Within Subjects Factors

If contrasts are requested on both between subjects factors and repeated measures factors in the same program, the repeated measures request comes first, with the request for contrasts on the between subjects factor following the first DESIGN subcommand, followed by a second DESIGN subcommand, as illustrated in Fig. 6.21.

Note that SIGNIF(UNIV) is again used as an added specification in the PRINT subcommand in Fig. 6.21, because one of the contrasts is for a repeated measures factor.

When contrasts are requested on both a between subjects factor, and a repeated measures factor, the printout includes interactions of the contrasts in special tables, described in the section on reading the printouts.

```
TITLE THREE FACTORS, ONE REPEATED MEASURE (C)
SUBTITLE CONTRASTS ON FACTORS A AND B
DATA LIST LIST/A B C1 C2 C3
MANOVA C1 C2 C3 BY A(1,3) B(1,4)
  /WSFACTORS = C(3)
  /PRINT = CELLINFO(MEANS)
  /DESIGN
  /CONTRAST(A) = SPECIAL(3*1, 1,0,-1, -1,2,-1)
  /CONTRAST(B) = SPECIAL(4*1, 3,-1,-1,-1, 0,0,1,-1 0,-2,1,1)
  /DESIGN = A(1) A(2) B(2) B(3)
BEGIN DATA
  .
  .
  .
```

FIG. 6.19.   Contrasts on both between subjects factors in a three factor mixed design.

```
TITLE THREE FACTORS, ONE REPEATED MEASURE (C)
SUBTITLE CONTRASTS ON FACTORS A AND B PLUS CONTRAST INTERACTIONS
DATA LIST LIST/A B C1 C2 C3
MANOVA C1 C2 C3 BY A(1,3) B(1,4)
  /WSFACTORS = C(3)
  /PRINT = CELLINFO(MEANS)
  /DESIGN
  /CONTRAST(A) = SPECIAL(3*1, 1,0,-1, -1,2,-1)
  /CONTRAST(B) = SPECIAL(4*1, 3,-1,-1,-1, 0,0,1,-1, 0,-2,1,1)
  /DESIGN = A(1) A(2) B(2) B(3) A(1) BY B A(2) BY B
BEGIN DATA
  .
  .
  .
```

FIG. 6.20.   Contrasts on both between subjects factors in a three factor mixed design, plus two interactions of contrasts with a second between subjects factor.

```
TITLE 2 FACTORS, ONE REPEATED MEASURE (C)
SUBTITLE CONTRASTS ON BOTH FACTORS
DATA LIST LIST/A C1 C2 C3
MANOVA C1 C2 C3 BY A(1,3)
    /WSFACTORS = C(3)
    /CONTRAST(C) = SPECIAL(3*1, 2, -1, -1, 0,1, -1)
    /RENAME = MEAN FIRST SECOND
    /PRINT = CELLINFO(MEANS) SIGNIF(UNIV)
    /DESIGN
    /CONTRAST(A) = SPECIAL(3*1, 1,0, -1, -1,2, -1)
    /DESIGN = A(1) A(2)
BEGIN DATA
    . .
    .
    .
```

FIG. 6.21.   Contrasts on both a repeated measures and a between subjects factor, in a two factor mixed design.

Extrapolation to Additional Factors and Contrasts

Extrapolation to more variables has been discussed throughout this chapter, but is summarized here, along with figure numbers of the relevant illustrations. Additional between subjects factors, if added to the design, do not change the programs; it is only necessary that the added variables be mentioned in the DATA LIST and MANOVA commands. Additional repeated measures only complicate the program by the requirement that the levels be combined in the DATA LIST and MANOVA commands. Additionally, care must be taken in the order of listing the repeated measures in the WSFACTORS subcommand (most slowly changing first). Also, if the RENAME subcommand is used, more names are required, equalling the number of combined levels of the repeated measures.

If contrasts are to be done on more than one between subjects factor, they are added with additional CONTRAST subcommands, consecutively placed, all preceding the *same* DESIGN subcommand (illustrated in Figs. 6.2, 6.4, and 6.19). This is also the case with contrasts on more than one repeated measures factor, where they would also follow each other (as illustrated in Figs. 6.11 and 6.16). Separation of CONTRAST requests by a DESIGN subcommand is only required when one of the requests is for a second set of contrasts on the same factor. Requests for two different sets of between subjects contrasts on the same factor are illustrated in Figs. 6.3 and 6.18. Requests for two different sets of repeated measures contrasts on the same factor are illustrated in Figs. 6.7 and 6.15. Figure 6.21 offers the example of requests for contrasts on both a between subjects and repeated measures factor.

SIMPLE EFFECTS OF CONTRASTS

In this chapter contrasts and interactions of contrasts have been discussed. A statistically significant interaction of a contrast with another factor indicates that the contrast yields different results at different levels of the second factor. For example, the contrast might be significant at one level, but not at another. Given a statistically significant interaction of a contrast with a factor, the next question is, at which levels will statistical significance be found? This requires a simple effect test at each level of the second factor. Figure 6.22 offers a program for a two factor completely randomized design, where one set of contrasts (on one factor) are requested, along

```
TITLE TWO BET. SUBJ. FACTORS, SIMPLE EFFECTS OF CONTRASTS
DATA LIST LIST/A B SCORE
MANOVA SCORE BY A(1,3) B(1,3)
  /CONTRAST(A)=SPECIAL(3*1, 1,0,-1, -1,2,-1)
  /PRINT=CELLINFO(MEANS)
  /DESIGN=A(1) A(2) A(1) BY B
  /DESIGN=A(1) WITHIN B(1) A(1) WITHIN B(2) A(1) WITHIN B(3)
  /DESIGN
BEGIN DATA
  .
  .
  .
```

FIG. 6.22.   Program for obtaining contrasts, the interaction of one contrast with a second factor, and the simple effects of one of the contrasts, in a two factor completely randomized design. A third DESIGN subcommand is added to yield the omnibus main effect F tests.

```
TITLE TWO FACTOR REPEATED MEASURE, SIMPLE EFFECTS OF CONTRASTS
DATA LIST LIST/B1C1 B1C2 B1C3 B2C1 B2C2 B2C3
 B3C1 B3C2 B3C3
MANOVA B1C1 B1C2 B1C3 B2C1 B2C2 B2C3 B3C1 B3C2 B3C3
  /WSFACTORS=B(3) C(3)
  /CONTRAST(B)=SPECIAL(3*1, 1,-1,0, -1,-1,2)
  /CONTRAST(C)=SPECIAL(3*1, -1,0,1, 1,-2,1)
  /RENAME=MEAN B1 B2 C1 C2 B1XC1 B1XC2 B2XC1 B2XC2
  /PRINT=CELLINFO(MEANS) SIGNIF(UNIV)
  /WSDESIGN
  /DESIGN
  /WSDESIGN=B(1) BY C
  /DESIGN
  /WSDESIGN=B WITHIN C(1) B WITHIN C(2) B WITHIN C(3)
  /DESIGN
BEGIN DATA
  .
  .
  .
```

FIG. 6.23.   Program for obtaining contrasts, the interaction of one contrast with a second factor, and the simple effects of one set of contrasts (B), in a two factor repeated measures design.

with the interaction of one of the contrasts with the second factor, and the simple effects of that contrast.

In Fig. 6.22 the first DESIGN subcommand, by including the specification A(1) BY B, requests the test of the interaction of the first contrast of A with factor B. The second DESIGN subcommand contains the specifications for the simple effects tests on the first contrast of A, with the A(1) WITHIN B(1), A(1) WITHIN B(2), and A(1) WITHIN B(3) specifications. The third DESIGN subcommand is not necessary for the simple effects, but is included so that the regular analysis of variance (the omnibus F tests of the main effects for the factors) is included.

Figure 6.23 offers a program for a two factor repeated measures design, which includes requests for simple effects of the contrasts of B.

In Fig. 6.23 there is a request for the test of the interaction of one contrast with a second factor, along with the tests of the simple effects of that contrast. A set of contrasts on the second factor are also requested, though there is no request for simple effects tests on this second set of contrasts.

Note that in Fig. 6.23 the specifications within the subcommands are different than in Fig. 6.22. For repeated measures factors the simple effects tests for contrasts should not specify the contrasts. That is, one would not ask for B(1) WITHIN C(1), but rather for B WITHIN C(1), as has been done within the second WSDESIGN subcommand in Fig. 6.23. If contrasts on a repeated measure are requested along with simple effects, then the

```
TITLE TWO FACTOR MIXED, CONTRASTS AND SIMPLE EFFECTS ON A
DATA LIST LIST/A C1 C2 C3
MANOVA C1 C2 C3 BY A(1,3)
   /WSFACTORS = C(3)
   /CONTRAST(C) = SPECIAL(3*1, 2, -1, -1, 0,1, -1)
   /RENAME = MEAN FIRST SECOND
   /PRINT = CELLINFO(MEANS) SIGNIF(UNIV)
   /WSDESIGN
   /DESIGN
   /CONTRAST(A) = SPECIAL(3*1, -1,0, -1, 1,2, -1)
   /DESIGN = A(1) A(2)
   /WSDESIGN = MWITHIN C(1) MWITHIN C(2) MWITHIN C(3)
   /DESIGN = A(1)
BEGIN DATA
    .
    .
    .
```

FIG. 6.24. Contrasts and simple effects on the between subjects factor (A) in a two factor mixed design. The printouts will present the requested contrasts of A, and the simple effects of the specified contrasts (contrasts A(1) and A(2) at specific levels of C, and tests of the interactions of the contrasts on A with C. A set of contrasts for factor C is specified, and interactions of these contrasts with the contrasts on A will be tested. If no contrasts are specified on the repeated measures factor, the program puts in its own contrasts and runs the interactions.

program does the simple effects tests of all of the contrasts on the repeated measure. Following the commands and subcommands of Fig. 6.23, each of the contrasts on B would be examined at the levels of C that were requested with the B WITHIN C(1), B WITHIN C(2), etc., specifications, seen within the third WSDESIGN subcommand. The subcommands preceding the first DESIGN subcommand in Fig. 6.23 are there to obtain a full analysis of variance, and to obtain main effect contrasts, prior to the simple effects contrasts that are requested later in the program.

Figures 6.24 and 6.25 also offer examples of programs combining contrasts and simple effects tests, but for mixed designs.

The program in Fig. 6.24 includes tests of the contrasts of the between subjects factor (A) that are restricted to specific levels of the repeated measures factor (C). The program in Fig. 6.25 includes tests of the contrasts of the repeated measures factor (C) that are restricted to specific levels of the between subjects factor (A).

Simple Effects of Interactions Between Contrasts

When working with a design that has more than two factors, questions can be asked about simple effects of interactions. For example, in a three factor mixed design with two repeated measures, there could be interest in the interaction between the contrasts on one repeated measure (C) and the

```
TITLE TWO FACTOR MIXED, CONTRASTS AND SIMPLE EFFECTS ON C
DATA LIST LIST/A C1 C2 C3
MANOVA C1 C2 C3 BY A(1,3)
   /WSFACTORS = C(3)
   /CONTRAST(C) = SPECIAL(3*1, 0,-1,1, 2,-1,-1)
   /RENAME = MEAN FIRST SECOND
   /PRINT = CELLINFO(MEANS) SIGNIF(UNIV)
   /WSDESIGN
   /DESIGN
   /WSDESIGN = C
   /DESIGN = MWITHIN A(1) MWITHIN A(2) MWITHIN A(3)
   /CONTRAST(A) = SPECIAL(3*1, 1,0,-1, -1,2,-1)
   /DESIGN = A(1) A(2)
BEGIN DATA
   .
   .
   .
```

FIG. 6.25.   Contrasts and simple effects on the repeated measures factor (C) in a two factor mixed design. The printouts will present the requested contrasts of C, the requested simple effects of C, and the simple effects of the contrasts, that is, the contrasts of C at specific levels of A. Tests of the interactions of the contrasts on C with the other factor are also run with this program. A set of contrasts for factor A is specified, and interactions of these contrasts with the contrasts on C will be tested. If no contrasts are specified on the between subjects factor, the program puts in its own contrasts and runs the interactions of contrasts.

```
TITLE THREE FACTORS, TWO REPEATED MEASURES (B & C)
SUBTITLE SIMPLE INTERACTION OF CONTRASTS ON A & C
DATA LIST LIST/A B1C1 B1C2 B1C3 B2C1 B2C2 B2C3 B3C1
  B3C2 B3C3
MANOVA B1C1 B1C2 B1C3 B2C1 B2C2 B2C3 B3C1 B3C2 B3C3 BY A(1,3)
  /WSFACTORS=B(3) C(3)
  /CONTRAST(B)=SPECIAL(3*1, -1,1,0, 1,1,-2)
  /CONTRAST(C)=SPECIAL(3*1, 1,0,-1, -1,2,-1)
  /RENAME=MEAN B1 B2 C1 C2 B1XC1 B1XC2 B2XC1 B2XC2
  /PRINT=CELLINFO(MEANS) SIGNIF(UNIV)
  /WSDESIGN
  /DESIGN
  /WSDESIGN=C WITHIN B(1) C WITHIN B(2)
  /DESIGN
  /CONTRAST(A)=SPECIAL(3*1, 0,1,-1, 2,-1,-1)
  /DESIGN=A(1) A(2)
BEGIN DATA
  .
  .
  .
```

FIG. 6.26.   Simple interaction of contrasts on mixed factors A & C at selected levels of a repeated measures factor B, in a three factor mixed design. The request for a set of contrasts on factor B is optional; the program would yield the desired simple interaction of contrasts without it.

```
TITLE THREE FACTORS, TWO REPEATED MEASURES (B & C)
SUBTITLE SIMPLE INTERACTION OF CONTRASTS ON B & C
DATA LIST LIST/A B1C1 B1C2 B1C3 B2C1 B2C2 B2C3 B3C1
  B3C2 B3C3
MANOVA B1C1 B1C2 B1C3 B2C1 B2C2 B2C3 B3C1 B3C2 B3C3 BY A(1,3)
  /WSFACTORS=B(3) C(3)
  /CONTRAST(B)=SPECIAL(3*1, -1,1,0, 1,1,-2)
  /CONTRAST(C)=SPECIAL(3*1, 1,0,-1, -1,2,-1)
  /RENAME=MEAN B1 B2 C1 C2 B1XC1 B1XC2 B2XC1 B2XC2
  /PRINT=CELLINFO(MEANS) SIGNIF(UNIV)
  /WSDESIGN
  /DESIGN
  /WSDESIGN=C BY B
  /DESIGN=MWITHIN A(1) MWITHIN A(2)
BEGIN DATA
  .
  .
  .
```

FIG. 6.27.   Simple interaction of contrasts on repeated measures factors B & C at selected levels of between subjects factor A, in a three factor mixed design.

between subjects factor (A), at a specific level of repeated measures factor B. Figure 6.26 offers an example of a program that would yield this simple interaction of contrasts.

If what was desired, was the interaction of the two repeated measures contrasts (B and C) at selected levels of the between subjects factor A, Fig. 6.27 would offer an appropriate program, assuming the same three factor design seen in Fig. 6.26.

In Fig. 6.27 the critical component for obtaining the simple effect of the interaction of two repeated measures contrasts, is specifying which interaction is desired, in the WSDESIGN subcommand.

For a three factor design with only one repeated measures factor, C, one might wish to look at the simple interaction of the two between subjects factors, at one level of the repeated measures factor. An appropriate program for this purpose is shown in Fig. 6.28.

It is critical, in the program in Fig. 6.28, that the specific interaction for the two between subjects factor contrasts be specified, as with A(1) BY B(2), along with the level of the third factor at which the simple effect is to be tested, as in MWITHIN C(1).

```
TITLE THREE FACTORS, ONE REPEATED MEASURE, C
SUBTITLE SIMPLE INTERACTION OF CONTRASTS ON A & B
DATA LIST LIST/A B C1 C2 C3 C4
MANOVA C1 C2 C3 C4 BY A(1,3) B(1,3)
  /WSFACTORS = C(4)
  /PRINT = CELLINFO(MEANS) SIGNIF(UNIV)
  /WSDESIGN
  /DESIGN
  /CONTRAST(A) = SPECIAL(3*1, 1,0,-1, -1,2,-1)
  /CONTRAST(B) = SPECIAL(3*1, 1,-1,0, 1,1,-2)
  /WSDESIGN = MWITHIN C(1)
  /DESIGN = A(1) A(2) B(1) B(2) A(1) BY B(2)
BEGIN DATA
  .
  .
  .
```

FIG. 6.28.   Simple interaction of contrasts on between subjects factors A & B at the first level of repeated measures factor C, in a three factor mixed design.

```
TITLE THREE FACTORS, ONE REPEATED MEASURE, C
SUBTITLE SIMPLE INTERACTION OF CONTRASTS ON A & C
DATA LIST LIST/A B C1 C2 C3 C4
MANOVA C1 C2 C3 C4 BY A(1,2) B(1,3)
  /WSFACTORS = C(4)
  /CONTRAST(C) = SPECIAL(4*1, -3,1,1,1, 0,0,1,-1, 0,-2,1,1)
  /RENAME = MEAN LINEAR QUADR CUBIC
  /PRINT = CELLINFO(MEANS) SIGNIF(UNIV)
  /WSDESIGN
  /DESIGN
  /CONTRAST(A) = SPECIAL(3*1, -1,0,1, -1,2,-1)
  /DESIGN = A(1) A(2)
  /DESIGN = A(1) WITHIN B(1) A(1) WITHIN B(2) A(2) WITHIN B(1)
    A(2) WITHIN B(2)
BEGIN DATA
  .
  .
  .
```

FIG. 6.29.   Simple interaction of contrasts on between subjects factor A and repeated measures factor C, at levels one and two of between subjects factor B, in a three factor mixed design.

Still assuming the design used in Fig. 6.28, that is, three factors with one repeated measures factor C, the interest could be in a simple interaction of contrasts on factors A and C (a mixed interaction). Specifically, assume that the interaction of the trends of factors A and C is to be examined at the first two levels of factor B. Figure 6.29 gives the correct program for this purpose, which also includes the main effects analysis.

SIMPLE SIMPLE EFFECTS OF CONTRASTS

In a three factor design, simple simple contrast effects can be needed. For example, in a three factor design with one repeated measure C, one might

```
TITLE THREE FACTORS, ONE REPEATED MEASURE, C
SUBTITLE SIMPLE SIMPLE CONTRASTS OF C
DATA LIST LIST/A B C1 C2 C3 C4
MANOVA C1 C2 C3 C4 BY A(1,2) B(1,3)
   /WSFACTORS = C(4)
   /CONTRAST(C) = SPECIAL(4*1, -3,1,1,1, 0,0,1,-1, 0,-2,1,1)
   /RENAME = MEAN FIRST SECOND THIRD
   /PRINT = CELLINFO(MEANS) SIGNIF(UNIV)
   /WSDESIGN
   /DESIGN
   /WSDESIGN = C
   /DESIGN = MWITHIN A(1) WITHIN B(1) MWITHIN A(1) WITHIN B(2)
BEGIN DATA
   .
   .
   .
```

FIG. 6.30.   Simple simple contrasts on the one repeated measure, C, in a three factor design.

```
TITLE THREE FACTORS, ONE REPEATED MEASURE, C
SUBTITLE SIMPLE SIMPLE CONTRAST OF B
DATA LIST LIST/A B C1 C2 C3 C4
MANOVA C1 C2 C3 C4 BY A(1,2) B(1,3)
   /WSFACTORS = C(4)
   /PRINT = CELLINFO(MEANS) SIGNIF(UNIV)
   /WSDESIGN
   /DESIGN
   /CONTRAST(B) = SPECIAL(3*1, 1,0,-1, -1,2,-1)
   /DESIGN = B(1) B(2)
   /WSDESIGN = MWITHIN C(1) MWITHIN C(2) MWITHIN C(3) MWITHIN C(4)
   /DESIGN = B(1) WITHIN A(1) B(2) WITHIN A(1)
BEGIN DATA
   .
   .
   .
```

FIG. 6.31.   Simple simple contrasts on one of the between subjects factors, B, restricted to the first level of A, examined within each of the levels of C, in a three factor design with one repeated measures factor, C.

```
TITLE THREE FACTORS, TWO REPEATED MEASURES, B & C
SUBTITLE SIMPLE SIMPLE CONTRASTS OF A
DATA LIST LIST/A B1C1 B1C2 B1C3 B2C1 B2C2 B2C3
MANOVA B1C1 B1C2 B1C3 B2C1 B2C2 B2C3 BY A(1,3)
   /WSFACTORS=B(2) C(3)
   /PRINT=CELLINFO(MEANS) SIGNIF(UNIV)
   /WSDESIGN
   /DESIGN
   /CONTRAST(A)=SPECIAL(3*1, -1,1,0, 1,1,-2)
   /DESIGN=A(1) A(2)
   /WSDESIGN=MWITHIN C(1) WITHIN B(1) MWITHIN C(1) WITHIN B(2)
   /DESIGN=A(1)
BEGIN DATA
   .
   .
   .
```

FIG. 6.32.   Simple simple contrasts on the between subjects factor, A, in a three factor design with two repeated measures (B & C). The first contrast of A is tested at the first level of C within each of the two levels of factor B.

```
TITLE THREE FACTOR DESIGN WITH TWO REPEATED MEASURES, B AND C
SUBTITLE SIMPLE SIMPLE CONTRASTS OF C
DATA LIST LIST/A B1C1 B1C2 B1C3 B2C1 B2C2 B2C3
MANOVA B1C1 B1C2 B1C3 B2C1 B2C2 B2C3 BY A(1,3)
   /WSFACTORS=B(2) C(3)
   /CONTRAST(C)=SPECIAL(3*1, 1,0,-1, 1,-2,1)
   /RENAME=MEAN B C1 C2 BXC1 BXC2
   /PRINT=CELLINFO(MEANS) SIGNIF(UNIV)
   /WSDESIGN
   /DESIGN
   /WSDESIGN=C WITHIN B(1) C WITHIN B(2)
   /DESIGN=MWITHIN A(1)
BEGIN DATA
   .
   .
   .
```

FIG. 6.33.   Simple simple contrasts on one of two repeated measures (C), in a three factor design. The contrasts of C are tested at the first level of A within the first and second levels of B.

wish to test the contrasts of C at the first level of A within both the first and second levels of B. Figure 6.30 offers a program that would yield such a test.

Assume that, for the same design, (three factors, one of which, C, is a repeated measure), what is desired is the following simple simple contrasts: each of the contrasts on factor B, restricted to the first level of A, examined within each of the levels of C. Figure 6.31 offers an appropriate program.

As another example, assume a three factor design with two repeated measures, B and C. Assume that the interest is in one of the contrasts of A restricted to the first level of C, examined at each of the levels of B. Figure 6.32 gives a program that would yield these tests. If simple simple contrasts on both A(1) and A(2) were desired, the last DESIGN subcommand in Fig. 6.32 would include reference to both contrasts, looking like the following:

```
/DESIGN=A(1) A(2)
```

Assume the same design again, that is, a three factor design with two repeated measures, B and C. Assume that the interest this time is in the contrasts of C restricted to the first level of A, within each of the two levels of B. Figure 6.33 gives a program that would yield these tests.

THE PRINTOUTS FOR CONTRASTS UNDER MANOVA

The contrasts for between subjects factors will always appear in similar tables, regardless of whether the design is a completely randomized or mixed design. Figure 6.34 offers an illustration of the test of one set of contrasts on a between subjects factor, in a two factor completely randomized design.

The error term in Fig. 6.34 is in the WITHIN CELLS row. The term SCORE in the heading refers to the dependent variable, and will be re-

```
* * * * * * * * * * ANALYSIS OF VARIANCE -- DESIGN   2 * * *
TESTS OF SIGNIFICANCE FOR SCORE USING UNIQUE SUMS OF SQUARES
SOURCE OF VARIATION        SS       DF        MS           F       SIG OF F

WITHIN CELLS             61.83       9       6.87
A(1)                     77.04       1      77.04        11.21       .009
A(2)                      1.12       1       1.12          .16       .695
```

FIG. 6.34. Between subjects factor contrasts, in a two factor completely randomized design.

```
* * * * * * * * * * * * * ANALYSIS OF VARIANCE -- DESIGN 1 * *

TESTS OF SIGNIFICANCE FOR SCORE USING UNIQUE SUMS OF SQUARES
SOURCE OF VARIATION         SS      DF        MS           F       SIG OF F

WITHIN CELLS              74.83      45       1.66
A(1)                       3.36       1       3.36         2.02       .162
A(2)                      17.12       1      17.12        10.30       .002
B(1)                     380.25       1     380.25       228.66       .000
B(2)                     412.23       1     412.23       247.89       .000
A(1) BY B                187.72       2      93.86        56.44       .000
A(2) BY B(1)               1.13       1       1.13          .68       .415
```

FIG. 6.35. Between subjects factors contrasts in a completely randomized design, where contrasts on both factors, plus the interaction of contrast A(1) with factor B, are tested, along with the interaction of the contrasts A(2) and B(1).

```
EFFECT .. C (CONT.)
UNIVARIATE F-TESTS WITH (1,3) D. F.

VARIABLE        HYPOTH. SS     ERROR SS      . . .             F      SIG. OF F

FIRST            64.00000       8.00000      . . .       24.00000        .016
SECOND           16.00000      24.00000      . . .        2.00000        .252
```

FIG. 6.36.   Test of a set of contrasts on a repeated measure, C, which has three levels, and in which the RENAME subcommand used the names FIRST and SECOND for the two contrasts. The central portion of the table, giving the mean squares, is not shown.

```
EFFECT .. B (CONT.)
UNIVARIATE F-TESTS WITH (1,5) D. F.

VARIABLE        HYPOTH. SS     ERROR SS      . . .             F      SIG. OF F

B1               93.44444      56.55556      . . .        8.26130        .035
B2               53.48148      25.18519      . . .       10.61765        .022
```

FIG. 6.37.   Test of two contrasts on a repeated measure A, in a two factor repeated measures design, where contrasts were requested on both repeated measures factors B and C (each containing three levels). The RENAME subcommand used the names MEANS B1 B2 C1 C2 B1XC1 B1XC2 B2XC1 B2XC2, under the assumption that B is the more slowly changing factor. The central portion of the table, giving the mean squares, is not shown.

placed by any other name that has been used for the dependent variable in the DATA LIST and MANOVA commands. The DESIGN number in the top-most heading changes as a function of which DESIGN subcommand follows the CONTRAST request. If there is more than one set of contrasts in the program on the same factor, they will appear in the printout in the same order as they were entered into the program (in different tables), each headed by the DESIGN number that follows the particular contrast request. (CONTRAST subcommands for the same factor are always separated by DESIGN subcommands.)

If there are CONTRAST requests on two or more between subjects factors, they will all appear in the same table, along with any requests for interactions between the contrasts, as seen in Fig. 6.35.

The tables for contrasts on repeated measures factors are different than those used for between subjects factors. Figure 6.36 offers an example of a table for contrasts in a single factor repeated measures design.

The tables are essentially the same when there is more than one repeated measures factor. The only variation is in the labels used for each row in the table, the labels coming from the names used for the contrasts and their interactions in the RENAME subcommand. Figure 6.37 offers a set of contrasts for factor B in a two factor repeated measures design where contrasts have been requested on both repeated measures factors B and C.

Figure 6.37 gives the contrasts on factor B. The contrasts on factor C would appear in a table identical to that seen in Fig. 6.37, except that the contrasts would be headed C1 and C2, instead of B1 and B2, given the names used in the RENAME subcommand (indicated in the legend for the figure).

The interaction of the contrasts of the two repeated measures would appear in a table like that seen in Fig. 6.38, where the heading EFFECT . . B BY C indicates that interactions concerning these two factors appear in the table.

In a mixed design the table for between subjects contrasts would look similar to those seen in Fig. 6.34 and 6.35, and for repeated measures contrasts would look similar to those presented in Fig. 6.36 through 6.38. However, with mixed designs, some tests for interactions between contrasts can appear in tables that look a little different. Figure 6.39 offers an example of the interaction between contrast A(1) of a between subjects factor A, and the contrast labeled FIRST on the repeated measures factor C, in a mixed design.

Figure 6.40 offers an illustration of a table for the interaction of each contrast of a repeated measured factor C, with the between subjects factor A, in a two factor mixed design. (Note that this is not a test of an interaction

```
EFFECT .. B BY C (CONT.)
UNIVARIATE F TESTS WITH (1,5) D. F.
```

VARIABLE	HYPOTH. SS	ERROR SS	. . .	F	SIG. OF F
B1XC1	2.66667	18.33333	. . .	.72727	.433
B1XC2	1.38889	3.61111	. . .	1.92308	.224
B2XC1	.05556	3.27778	. . .	.08475	.783
B2XC2	.29630	7.03704	. . .	.21053	.666

FIG. 6.38. The interaction of contrasts, in a two factor repeated measures design, where the two factors each have three levels. The names (B1XC1, B1XC2, etc.) are those given in the RENAME subcommand. If B is the most slowly changing variable, then the interactions, in the order given, would be B1 × C1, B1 × C2, B2 × C1, and B2 × C2. The central portion of the table, giving the mean squares, is not shown.

```
EFFECT .. A(1) BY C (CONT.)
UNIVARIATE F-TESTS WITH (1,9) D. F.
```

VARIABLE	HYPOTH. SS	ERROR SS	. . .	F	SIG. OF F
FIRST	7.52083	6.29167	. . .	10.75828	.010
SECOND	1.56250	14.37500	. . .	.97826	.348

FIG. 6.39. Interaction of each repeated measures contrast with a specified contrast on a between subjects factor. The first test, labeled FIRST (if the name FIRST was used in the RENAME subcommand), is a test of whether the first contrast of repeated measures factor C interacts with the contrast on the between subjects factor that had been labeled A(1) in the DESIGN subcommand. The central portion of the table, giving the mean squares, is not shown.

```
EFFECT .. A BY C (CONT.)
UNIVARIATE F-TESTS WITH (2,9) D. F.
```

VARIABLE	HYPOTH. SS	ERROR SS	. . .	F	SIG. OF F
FIRST	8.08333	6.29167	. . .	5.78146	.024
SECOND	5.08333	14.37500	. . .	1.59130	.256

FIG. 6.40. Interaction of each contrast of a repeated measures factor C, with the between subjects factor A, in a two factor mixed design. The names FIRST and SECOND were used in the RENAME subcommand to designate the first and second contrasts on C. In the table, each test is a test of whether the particular contrast of C (for example, FIRST), is different at the different levels of factor A. The central portion of the table, giving the mean squares, is not shown.

```
* * * * * * * * * * * * ANALYSIS OF VARIANCE -- DESIGN  2 * *
TESTS INVOLVING 'C' WITHIN-SUBJECT EFFECT
```

AVERAGED TESTS OF SIGNIF FOR C USING UNIQUE SUMS OF SQUARES

SOURCE OF VARIATION	SS	DF	MS	F	SIG OF F
WITHIN CELLS	20.67	18	1.15		
C	118.17	2	59.08	51.45	.000
A(1) BY C	9.08	2	4.54	3.96	.038
A(2) BY C	4.08	2	2.04	1.78	.197

FIG. 6.41. Test of significance for repeated measures factor C, and tests of whether the contrasts A(1) and A(2) of the between subjects factor A interact with repeated measures factor C.

```
* * * * * * * * * * * ANALYSIS OF VARIANCE -- DESIGN 2 * * * * *
TESTS OF SIGNIFICANCE FOR SCORE USING UNIQUE SUMS OF SQUARES
```

SOURCE OF VARIATION	SS	DF	MS	F	SIG OF F
WITHIN CELLS	74.83	45	1.66		
A(1) WITHIN B(1)	3.00	1	3.00	1.80	.186
A(1) WITHIN B(2)	140.08	1	140.08	84.24	.000
A(1) WITHIN B(3)	48.00	1	48.00	24.86	.000

FIG. 6.42. Simple contrasts in a two factor completely randomized design. A(1) is a contrast on factor A, and B(1), B(2), and B(3) are the levels of factor B at which the contrast on A is being tested.

```
EFFECT .. B WITHIN C(1) (CONT.)
UNIVARIATE F-TESTS WITH (1,5) D. F.
```

VARIABLE	HYPOTH. SS	ERROR SS	. . .	F	SIG OF F
B1	3.00000	4.00000	. . .	3.75000	.111
B2	40.11111	38.22222	. . .	5.24709	.071

FIG. 6.43. Table showing a test of the simple effects of two contrasts on factor B, at the first level of factor C, in a design where both factors B and C are repeated measures. The labels for each row (B1 and B2 in this example) are not necessarily the labels that would appear in the table. See the text for a further explanation of these row labels.

```
* * * * * * * * * * ANALYSIS OF VARIANCE -- DESIGN  3 * * * *
TESTS INVOLVING 'MWITHIN C(1) WITHIN-SUBJECT EFFECT.
SOURCE OF VARIATION          SS        DF        MS           F        SIG OF F

WITHIN CELLS               24.75        9       2.75
MWITHIN C(1)              126.75        1     126.75        42.09        .000
A(1) BY MWITHIN C(1)        8.00        1       8.00         2.91        .122
```

FIG. 6.44.   Table showing a test of the simple effect of one contrast on factor A, at the first level of repeated measures factor C, in a two factor mixed design. The WITHIN CELLS row offers the error term. The numerator in the F ratio, and the F test itself, are found in the row A(1) by MWITHIN C(1). The middle row is not relevant for this design. Separate tables would offer the tests for the different levels of factor C.

```
EFFECT .. MWITHIN A(1) BY C (CONT.)
UNIVARIATE F-TESTS WITH (1,9) D. F.

VARIABLE        HYPOTH. SS       ERROR SS    . . .           F        SIG OF F

FIRST           18.16667         6.29167     . . .       11.68212        .008
SECOND          12.50000        14.37500     . . .        7.82609        .021
```

FIG. 6.45.   Simple effects of the contrasts on repeated measures factor C in a two factor mixed design. In this table the two contrasts on factor C (FIRST and SECOND) are each tested within the first level of factor A. Separate tables give the tests at the different levels of factor A. MWITHIN is a keyword in SPSS-XX, which can be read as "within" for the mixed design case. Thus the table heading can be read as C WITHIN A(1), in a mixed design.

```
EFFECT .. MWITHIN A(1) WITHIN B(1) BY C (CONT.)
UNIVARIATE F-TESTS WITH (1,54) D. F.

VARIABLE        HYPOTH. SS       ERROR SS    . . .           F        SIG OF F

FIRST             .17857        45.35714     . . .         .21260        .647
SECOND          34.32143        84.35714     . . .       21.97036        .000
THIRD            4.46429        49.50000     . . .        4.87013        .032
```

FIG. 6.46.   Simple simple effects of the contrasts on repeated measures factor C in a three factor mixed design, with one repeated measure, C. In this table the three contrasts on factor C (FIRST, SECOND and THIRD) are each tested within the first level of factor A at the first level of factor B. Separate tables give the tests at the different levels of factor B that were requested in the program (presented in this chapter in Fig. 6.30).

between two contrasts, but, in each case, is a test of the interaction of a contrast on a repeated measure C, with a between subjects factor A; asking whether each contrast on C is different at the different levels of A.)

The principle headings in Fig. 6.38 and 6.40 have a similar appearance, but do not refer to the same tests. In Fig. 6.40 the factors in the table heading, EFFECT . . A BY C, are mixed, and the row labels refer to the contrasts for the repeated measures factor. In Fig. 6.38, the factors in the table heading EFFECT B BY C, are both repeated measures, and the row labels refer to interactions between contrasts on the two factors.

Figure 6.41 offers a table of tests of whether the contrasts of the between subjects factor A interact with the repeated measures factor C, in a two factor mixed design.

Whereas Fig. 6.41 offers a table for the interaction of a between subjects factor's contrast with a repeated measures factor, Fig. 6.40 offers a table for the interaction of a repeated measures factor's contrast with a between subject's factor.

Tables for Simple Contrasts

Figure 6.42 offers a table illustrating simple effects of contrasts on a between subjects factor. A program that would produce such a table is seen in Fig. 6.22 of this chapter.

Figure 6.43 offers a table illustrating the simple effects of repeated measures contrasts. A program that would produce such a table is seen in Fig. 6.23 of this chapter.

The names in the RENAME subcommand used in the illustrative program seen in Fig. 6.23 would guide you through the printout for the regular contrasts and their interactions. However, these RENAME labels would not be helpful for the simple contrasts. For the simple contrasts, you have to recognize the different contrasts by the order in which they appear in the table, the first row refering to the first contrast, the second row to the second contrast. The table heading B WITHIN C(1) indicates that these

```
* * * * * * * * * * * ANALYSIS OF VARIANCE -- DESIGN  2 * * * *
TESTS INVOLVING 'MWITHIN C(1)' WITHIN-SUBJECT EFFECT.

TESTS OF SIGNIFICANCE FOR T1 USING UNIQUE SUMS OF SQUARES
SOURCE OF VARIATION          SS        DF        MS          F        SIG OF F

WITHIN CELLS               70.57       54       1.31
MWITHIN C(1)              396.25        1      396.25      303.21       .000
B(1) WITHIN A(1) BY         2.38        1        2.38        1.82       .183
MWITHIN C(1)
B(2) WITHIN A(1) BY         1.17        1        1.17         .89       .349
MWITHIN C(1)
```

FIG. 6.47. Simple simple effects of a contrast on between subjects factor B in a three factor mixed design, with one repeated measure, C. In this table, both the first contrast on factor B, labeled B(1), and the second contrast, labeled B(2), are tested within the first level of A and the first level of C, yielding F values of 1.82 and .89, respectively. The row labeled MWITHIN C(1) is not meaningful for this design. The presence of the word BY in the row labels indicate the rows offering the requested tests. Separate tables are used for the different levels of C at which the B contrasts are tested.

```
* * * * * * * * * * ANALYSIS OF VARIANCE -- DESIGN 2 * * * *
TESTS INVOLVING 'MWITHIN C(1) WITHIN B(1)' WITHIN-SUBJECT EFFECT.
```

```
TESTS OF SIGNIFICANCE FOR T1 USING UNIQUE SUMS OF SQUARES
```

SOURCE OF VARIATION	SS	DF	MS	F	SIG OF F
WITHIN CELLS	12.67	6	2.11		
MWITHIN C(1) WITHIN B(1)	87.11	1	87.11	41.25	.001
A(1) BY MWITHIN C(1) WITHIN B(1)	8.17	1	8.17	3.87	.097

FIG. 6.48. Simple simple effect of a contrast on between subjects factor A in a three factor mixed design, with two repeated measures, B and C. In this table the first contrast on factor A, labeled A(1), is tested within the first level of B and the first level of C, yielding an F value of 3.87. The presence of the word BY in the row label indicates the row with the desired F test. The row labeled WITHIN CELLS presents the error term for the F ratio. The middle row is not relevant for this design. Separate tables are used for the different levels of B at which the A contrasts are tested. If simple simple contrasts on both A contrasts, A(1) and A(2), were requested, they would appear in the same table.

```
EFFECT .. MWITHIN A(1) BY C WITHIN B(1) (CONT.)
UNIVARIATE F-TESTS WITH (1,6) D. F.
```

VARIABLE	HYPOTH. SS	ERROR SS	. . .	F	SIG OF F
B	48.16667	3.66667	. . .	78.81818	.000
C1	1.38889	4.33333	. . .	1.925308	.215

FIG. 4.49. Simple simple effects of the contrasts on repeated measures factor C in a three factor mixed design, with two repeated measures, B and C. In this table the two contrasts on factor C are each tested within the first level of factor A at the first level of factor B. Separate tables give the tests at the different levels of factor B that were requested in the program presented in this chapter in Fig. 6.31. The row labels, B and C1, can vary, and so may not be informative in this case, and could be any of the labels used in the RENAME subcommand. The different contrasts for factor C are distinguished by their placement. The first (uppermost) row refers to the first contrast on C, and the second row to the second contrast on C, regardless of the row labels.

are the contrasts concerning factor B, at the first level of factor C. Different tables would be used for each level of C.

Figure 6.44 offers a table for the simple effects of the contrasts on the between subjects factor, A, in a two factor mixed design. (Figure 6.24 in this chapter offers a program that would produce such a table.)

Figure 6.45 offers a table for the simple effects of the contrasts on a repeated measures factor C in a two factor mixed design. Figure 6.25 in this chapter presents a program that would produce a table like that illustrated in Fig. 6.45.

Tables for Simple Simple Contrasts

Figure 6.46 offers a table indicating some simple simple effects of a repeated measures factor, C, in a three factor design with one repeated measure (C).

Figure 6.47 illustrates a table offering some simple simple effects of contrasts on one of the between subjects factors, B, in a three factor design with one repeated measure, C. A program that would produce such a table is seen in Fig. 6.31 in this chapter.

Figure 6.48 offers a table for some simple simple effects of the between subjects factor A in a three factor mixed design with two repeated measures, B and C. Figure 6.32 of this chapter offers a program that would produce such a table.

Figure 6.49 offers a table for simple simple effects of the repeated measures factor C in a three factor mixed design with two repeated measures, B and C. Figure 6.33 of this chapter offers a program that would produce such a table.

7 Trend Analysis

A trend analysis can be understood as a test of a specific contrast. Therefore, in SPSS, the programs for trend analyses are included as an optional specification within the programs for contrasts. For this reason the programs for trend analyses are similar to the programs for contrasts under MANOVA. Some of the verbalization in this chapter will therefore be similar to what appears in Chapter 6. The material is restated so that it will not be necessary to read both chapters when only doing a trend analysis, or only doing a special contrast.

COMPLETELY RANDOMIZED DESIGNS

The request for a trend analysis is initiated in a CONTRAST subcommand under MANOVA, as seen below in Fig. 7.1, which contains a program for a trend analysis in a one factor completely randomized design. (The factor is called A, and has four levels, and the dependent variable is called SCORE. The TITLE command is not necessary for the running of the program, and the details in the title have no influence on the program.)

The CONTRAST subcommand requires the use of the keyword POLYNOMIAL when a trend analysis is desired. The specific trends (linear, quadratic, etc.) are labeled within the DESIGN subcommand. As seen in Fig. 7.1, in the DESIGN subcommand, each trend must be designated by the numbers 1, 2, etc., in parentheses, each following the factor name. The number of such specifications must equal one less than the number of levels of the factor, since that is the number of trends that will be tested. For example, with four levels, the linear, quadratic, and cubic trends would

```
TITLE ONE FACTOR COMPLETELY RANDOMIZED, TREND ANALYSIS
DATA LIST LIST/A SCORE
MANOVA SCORE BY A(1,4)
  /CONTRAST(A) = POLYNOMIAL
  /PRINT = CELLINFO(MEANS)
  /DESIGN = A(1) A(2) A(3)
BEGIN DATA
  .
  .
  .
```

FIG. 7.1. Trend analysis in a one factor completely randomized design.

each be tested, requiring A(1), A(2), and A(3) following the equals sign in the DESIGN subcommand. In the printout, the test of the linear trend will be labeled A(1), the test of the quadratic trend A(2), etc.

The values for the levels of the trend factor in a trend analysis are important. For example, the factor could be number of milligrams of a drug, with the dosages being .5, 1.0, 1.5 and 2.0 milligrams. Note that these four dosages are each separated by .5 milligrams. If the intervals are all identical, the values for the individual intervals do not have to be specified. The example in Fig. 7.1 is written for the assumption of equal intervals. When no specific metric is specified, equal intervals are assumed. If the intervals are not equal their values must be specified within parentheses. For example,

```
MANOVA SCORE BY A(1,4)
  /CONTRAST(A) = POLYNOMIAL(1,2,2.5,3)
```

would be appropriate if the dosages were 1, 2, 2.5 and 3 milligrams.

To obtain the usual omnibus F test in addition to the trend analysis, add a DESIGN subcommand without an equals sign and without further specifications. This additional DESIGN subcommand can immediately precede, or immediately follow, the DESIGN subcommand with the specifications. This is illustrated in Fig. 7.2.

In a two factor completely randomized design the subcommands concerning the trend analysis are identical to those used within a one factor completely randomized design. This is illustrated in Fig. 7.3.

For the onmibus F tests of factors A and B and their interaction in

```
  .
  .
  .
  /DESIGN = A(1) A(2) A(3)
  /DESIGN
BEGIN DATA
  .
  .
  .
```

FIG. 7.2. Change in Fig. 7.1 required to include the omnibus F test.

```
TITLE TWO FACTOR COMPLETELY RANDOMIZED DESIGN, FACTORS A & B .
SUBTITLE TREND TEST ON FACTOR A
DATA LIST LIST/A B SCORE
MANOVA SCORE BY A(1,4) B(1,3)
   /CONTRAST(A) = POLYNOMIAL
   /PRINT = CELLINFO(MEANS)
   /DESIGN = A(1) A(2) A(3)
BEGIN DATA
   .
   .
   .
```

FIG. 7.3.   Trend analysis on one factor in a two factor completely randomized design.

```
TITLE TWO FACTOR COMPLETELY RANDOMIZED DESIGN
SUBTITLE TREND TESTS ON BOTH FACTORS
DATA LIST LIST/A B SCORE
MANOVA SCORE BY A(1,4) B(1,3)
   /CONTRAST(A) = POLYNOMIAL
   /CONTRAST(B) = POLYNOMIAL
   /PRINT = CELLINFO(MEANS)
   /DESIGN = A(1) A(2) A(3) B(1) B(2)
BEGIN DATA
   .
   .
   .
```

FIG. 7.4.   Trend tests on both factors in a two factor completely randomized design.

addition to the trend analysis, add a DESIGN subcommand without specifications, on the line following, or the line preceding, the DESIGN subcommand that has specifications.

If trend analyses are desired on both factors, add a second contrast request immediately following the first one, and extend the specifications in the DESIGN subcommand, in the manner illustrated in Fig. 7.4.

Note that the labels for the linear and quadratic trends on factor B are B(1) and B(2). If this second factor was called, say, TRTMT, the linear and quadratic trends for this second factor would be labeled TRTMT(1) and TRTMT(2), respectively.

The programs in Figs. 7.3 and 7.4 are also appropriate for completely randomized designs with more than two factors (with the naming of the additional factors in the MANOVA and DATA LIST commands). The SUBTITLE command in Figs. 7.3 and 7.4, like the TITLE command, is optional and has no effect on the running of the program; it merely provides for an additional line of headings on the printout pages.

Interactions of Trend Tests for Between Subjects Factors

There can also be interest in the interaction of a particular trend with the other factor. For example, there could be interest in the interaction of the linear trend of A with factor B. If the interaction of the linear trend of A with factor B was statistically significant, it would mean that there are different linear trends of A at the different levels of B, or linear trends of A at some levels of B, but not at others. To test this interaction, the specification A(1) by B would be added to the other specifications in the DESIGN subcommand in Fig. 7.4. Thus, the DESIGN subcommand would look like the following:

```
/DESIGN = A(1) A(2) A(3) B(1) B(2) A(1) BY B
```

There are other possible interactions of interest. For example, there could be interest in the interaction of two trends. Specifically, if the interaction of the linear trend of A with the linear trend of B was statistically significant, it would mean that the linear trend of A increases (or decreases) linearly over levels of B. This would be tested with the specification A(1) BY B(1). All such further specifications would be added to the DESIGN subcommand. The only requirement is that the total of all degrees of freedom for interaction questions being tested should not add up to more than the number of degrees of freedom in the interaction term. In the example in Fig. 7.4, with three and four levels of the factors, only six degrees of freedom could be called upon for interaction tests. An example of the DESIGN subcommand that includes requests for some trend interactions is seen in the following:

```
/DESIGN = A(1) A(2) A(3) B(1) B(2) A(1) BY B(1) A(2) BY B(1)
   A(3) BY B(1)
```

REPEATED MEASURES DESIGNS

When working with repeated measures, the WSFACTORS subcommand must follow the MANOVA command. As usual, the DESIGN subcommand is included as the last subcommand. To request a trend analysis, a CONTRAST subcommand follows the WSFACTORS subcommand. The RENAME subcommand can also be used, to aid in reading the printouts. The RENAME subcommand is included in the illustration of a trend test on a one factor repeated measures design, in Fig. 7.5

If the RENAME subcommand is used it is necessary to have as many names as there are levels. Although there will be one less trend analysis than the number of levels (two trends if three levels, three trends if four levels, etc.), the program requires a set of ones for an additional contrast, which has to be named. Thus some neutral name, such as MEAN or CONSTANT should be used for the first name, to identify this set of equal weights, along with meaningful names for the actual trend analyses. The

```
TITLE ONE FACTOR REPEATED MEASURES DESIGN, TREND TEST
DATA LIST LIST/C1 C2 C3 C4
MANOVA C1 C2 C3 C4
  /WSFACTORS = C(4)
  /CONTRAST(C) = POLYNOMIAL
  /RENAME = MEAN LINEAR QUADR CUBIC
  /PRINT = CELLINFO(MEANS) SIGNIF(UNIV)
  /DESIGN
BEGIN DATA
  .
  .
  .
```

FIG. 7.5.   Trend tests in a one factor repeated measures design.

names suggested are LINEAR, QUADR (the printout will only print the
first eight letters of any name, and QUADRATIC has nine), CUBIC,
QUARTIC, etc.

Note that, in Fig. 7.5 on the PRINT subcommand line, the additional
specification SIGNIF(UNIV) is added. This is needed to provide the univariate tests of the trend tests on a repeated measure in the printouts. For
any trend requests involving repeated measures the SIGNIF(UNIV) specification should be added to the PRINT subcommand. The program in Fig.
7.5 will yield the omnibus F test of factor C, as well as a trend analysis.

The CONTRAST subcommand as given in Fig. 7.5 is appropriate for
equal intervals between the levels of the factor being tested for a trend.
For example, the factor being tested for a trend might be numbers of bits
of information, and might be 2, 4, 6, and 8. As previously suggested in
the opening section of this chapter, if the intervals between levels are not
equal, their values must be specified, within parentheses. For example, if
the bits of information in each level were double the preceding level, as
in 2, 4, 8, 16, the intervals would no longer be equal. The appropriate
specification would then be as follows:

```
MANOVA C1 C2 C3 C4
  /WSFACTORS = C(4)
  /CONTRAST(C) = POLYNOMIAL(2,4,8,16)
```

Multiple Repeated Measures and Interactions of Trends

If there are two or more repeated measures in a design, the levels of the
different repeated measures must all be combined in the DATA LIST and
MANOVA commands. For example, given two repeated measures, B,
with two levels, and C, with three levels, the two factors would be combined
into six levels, possibly labeled B1C1 B1C2 B1C3 B2C1 B2C2 B3C3, if
the data were entered with factor B changing more slowly, as discussed in

Chapter Two. Recall that, if the RENAME subcommand is used it requires that there be as many labels as there are levels of the repeated measures factor. With two (or more) repeated measures factors the levels are combined as just described, so the RENAME subcommand will have as many labels as levels are produced by combining all of the repeated measures. If there are j levels of one factor, and k levels of the other factor, there will be a total of j times k measurements (combined levels). A concrete example is seen in Fig. 7.6, which offers a program for a test of the trends on factor C in a two factor repeated measures design.

The RENAME subcommand in Fig. 7.6 has six names, because the two factors have two times three equals six levels. The selection of the names in the RENAME subcommand is not arbitrary, although the program will accept any names that are entered, as long as they do not include more than eight letters. The first name is not important, because it only refers to a contrast of ones (and not one of the trends of interest). The second name refers to the most slowly changing factor (B here). The third and fourth names refer to the linear and quadratic trends being tested. The printout will have the labels LINEAR and QUADR next to the desired trend tests on factor C, if the RENAME subcommand has these specifications.

The last group of names in the RENAME subcommand in Fig. 7.6 refer to the interactions between the trends on C and trends on B, if such trends are requested. If no trends are requested on the second factor (as in this example), the program imposes its own test weights for contrasts. With only two levels on the second factor (B), the imposed contrast weights are 1, −1, making the the interaction of a trend of C and a contrast of B equivalent to the question of whether the linear trend of C is different at the two levels of factor B. That is why the label BXLC is used. BXQC is the label for the same question about the quadratic trend of C.

Assume, however, that there are more than two levels for the second factor. An example of this is seen in Fig. 7.7, which illustrates the proper

```
TITLE TWO REPEATED MEASURES, TESTING ONE FOR TRENDS
DATA LIST LIST/B1C1 B1C2 B1C3 B2C1 B2C2 B2C3
MANOVA B1C1 B1C2 B1C3 B2C1 B2C2 B2C3
  /WSFACTORS = B(2) C(3)
  /CONTRAST(C) = POLYNOMIAL
  /RENAME = MEAN B LINEAR QUADR BXLC BXQC
  /PRINT = CELLINFO(MEANS) SIGNIF(UNIV)
  /DESIGN
BEGIN DATA
       .
       .
       .
```

FIG. 7.6. Test of trends on one of two repeated measures in a two factor design with two repeated measures.

```
TITLE TWO REPEATED MEASURES, TESTING BOTH FOR TRENDS
DATA LIST LIST/B1C1 B1C2 B1C3 B2C1 B2C2 B2C3 B3C1
  B3C2 B3C3
MANOVA B1C1 B1C2 B1C3 B2C1 B2C2 B2C3 B3C1 B3C2 B3C3
  /WSFACTORS = B(3) C(3)
  /CONTRAST(B) = POLYNOMIAL
  /CONTRAST(C) = POLYNOMIAL
  /RENAME = MEAN LB QB LC QC LBXLC LBXQC QBXLC QBXQC
  /PRINT = CELLINFO(MEANS) SIGNIF(UNIV)
  /DESIGN
BEGIN DATA
  .
  .
  .
```

FIG. 7.7. Test of trends on both of the factors in a two factor repeated measures design.

program for obtaining trend tests on both of the repeated measures factors (in a two factor repeated measures design in which both factors have three levels).

The choice and placement of the names in the RENAME subcommand needs an explanation. As usual, the first name, MEAN, does not refer to useful information. The second through the fifth names, LB, QB, LC, and QC, specify the four requested trends (the linear and quadratic trends of both B and C). All of the trends on the most slowly changing factor are always represented first. The labels LBXLC LBXQC QBXLC QBXQC specify which interactions of trends are being tested. (These are all interactions of trends, not just interactions of trends and contrasts, because the keyword POLYNOMIAL requests a contrast that is a trend test.) Assuming that these labels are used in the suggested order, they will appear next to the appropriate interactions in the printout. The interactions will appear with the most slowly changing factor interacting first, that factor remaining until interactions with all levels of the other factor have been represented. The following statement summarizes the order of labels within the RENAME subcommand: the first name refers to the contrast of ones. The next j-1 names refer to the trends on the most slowly changing factor (which has j levels). The next k-1 names refer to the k-1 trends on the next most slowly changing factor (which has k levels). If there is a third repeated measures factor, its position is determined by which factors change before it and after it.

If there were five levels of the most slowly changing factor, and three of another factor, then the first four labels following MEAN would refer to the trends on the most slowly changing factor, and the next two to the trends on the other factor. The last few labels would refer to the interactions of the trends. Still assuming five levels of one factor and three of the other, among the five times three equals fifteen labels, there would be four, times two, equals eight interactions of trends represented. In general, given two factors with j and k levels, there will be (j-1) (k-1) interactions tested, so the last (j-1) (k-1) labels will refer to interactions.

Given two repeated measures factors, the program will impose contrasts on any factor for which trends or contrasts are not requested, and will use these imposed contrasts for computing the interactions of the trends with the contrasts. These terms can be ignored in the printout unless the user is interested in particular contrast interactions, in which case the user should select the contrasts. Interactions of trends and contrasts are discussed in a later section of this chapter.

The order in which the CONTRAST subcommands are given (that is, whether B or C is requested first) is not important. In Fig. 7.7, where the request for trend tests on C precedes the request for trend tests on B, the order of the requests could have been reversed without affecting the program. The order is only crucial within the WSFACTORS subcommand, where the most slowly changing factor must be first.

The Interaction of a Trend with Another Factor. In the preceding paragraphs, the discussion concerned trend interactions and interactions of trends and contrasts. A different question concerning trends is the question of whether the trend on one factor, say the linear trend, is different at different levels of another factor. This was alluded to before in regard to Fig. 7.6. Assume that, for the program in Fig. 7.7, there was a question of whether there is a significant interaction of the linear trend of B with factor C. To answer this question with two repeated measures, the WSDESIGN subcommand must be added to the program, along with some specifications. The WSDESIGN subcommand must follow the CONTRAST subcommand, but precede the DESIGN subcommand. For the program in Fig. 7.7, the added specifications for testing the interaction of the linear trend of B with factor C would produce the following program statement:

```
/WSDESIGN = B(1) BY C
```

The use of a parenthesized (1) following the name of the trend factor identifies the linear trend. If the interaction of interest concerned the quadratic trend of B with factor C, then

```
/WSDESIGN = B(2) BY C
```

would be appropriate.

Recall that the same specification was used in the DESIGN subcommand for between subjects factors. All such specifications for between subjects factors are made in the DESIGN subcommand; all such specifications for within subjects factors are made in the WSDESIGN subcommand.

A problem in adding specifications to the WSDESIGN subcommand, is that the *only* within subject analyses that are done, are those requested in the WSDESIGN subcommand, unless it is omitted, in which case a full analysis is done. If the WSDESIGN subcommand appears with specifications, then it should also appear without specifications, to obtain the usual full factorial analysis of variance (omnibus main effects and interaction tests), in addition to the specified additional analyses. An efficient way to do this, is to present the WSDESIGN subcommand with its added specifications after a request for the omnibus F tests. This can be done by presenting a WSDESIGN subcommand without specifications before the first DESIGN subcommand (but following the WSFACTORS and CONTRAST subcommands). An example is seen in Fig. 7.8, where the second WSDESIGN subcommand has the specifications C(1) BY B C(2) BY B, which are requests for the interactions of both the linear and quadratic trends of C with factor B. (If the full factorial analysis was not desired, then the first WSDESIGN and the first DESIGN subcommands would both be omitted from Fig. 7.8.)

Summary of Trend Interaction Tests Comparing Completely Randomized with Repeated Measures Designs

In summary, SPSS treats between and within subjects factors differently in regard to trend interactions. Given two between subjects factors, and trend requests for both, all interactions involving trends have to be specifically requested on the DESIGN subcommand, or they are not com-

```
TITLE TWO REPEATED MEASURES, TESTING BOTH FOR TRENDS
SUBTITLE ADDING AN INTERACTION SPECIFICATION
DATA LIST LIST/B1C1 B1C2 B1C3 B2C1 B2C2 B2C3 B3C1
 B3C2 B3C3
MANOVA B1C1 B1C2 B1C3 B2C1 B2C2 B2C3 B3C1 B3C2 B3C3
 /WSFACTORS=B(3) C(3)
 /CONTRAST(B)=POLYNOMIAL
 /CONTRAST(C)=POLYNOMIAL
 /RENAME=MEAN LB QB LC QC LBXLC LBXQC QBXLC QBXQC
 /PRINT=CELLINFO(MEANS) SIGNIF(UNIV)
 /WSDESIGN
 /DESIGN
 /WSDESIGN=C(1) BY B C(2) BY B
 /DESIGN
BEGIN DATA
 .
 .
 .
```

FIG. 7.8.   Test of trends on both of the factors in a two factor repeated measures design. A request for a test of the interaction of each trend of C with factor B has been added, using a second WSDESIGN subcommand.

puted. Given two repeated measures factors, and trend requests for both, the interactions of the requested trends will automatically appear in the printout. The only ones that have to be requested (if they are desired) are the interactions of each trend with another factor, and these have to be requested on the WSDESIGN subcommand, when working with repeated measures.

MIXED DESIGNS

In mixed designs requests for trends on repeated measures follow the form seen in prior sections. Examples in the context of mixed designs are offered below.

Trend Tests on Repeated Measures Factors in Mixed Designs

Figure 7.9 offers an example of a program for a test of a trend on a repeated measure (C) in a two factor mixed design.

As can be seen by comparing Figs. 7.5 and 7.9, the only change when adding a between subjects factor is in the DATA LIST and MANOVA commands, where the between subjects factor has to be named. The same program as that seen in Fig. 7.9 would be used for a design in which there were additional between subjects factors, requiring only the addition of the names of the other between subjects factors in the DATA LIST and MANOVA commands. The program remains essentially the same with added repeated measures. The only complications that arise are in the names for the optional RENAME subcommand, as discussed in the prior section on trends with multiple repeated measures. Figure 7.10 offers an example of a three factor design with two repeated measures, and a trend test on one repeated measure.

```
TITLE TWO FACTOR MIXED DESIGN, ONE REPEATED MEASURE C, TREND OF C
DATA LIST LIST/A C1 C2 C3 C4
MANOVA C1 C2 C3 C4 BY A(1,3)
   /WSFACTORS = C(4)
   /CONTRAST(C) = POLYNOMIAL
   /RENAME = MEAN LINEAR QUADR CUBIC
   /PRINT = CELLINFO(MEANS) SIGNIF(UNIV)
   /DESIGN
BEGIN DATA
   .
   .
   .
```

FIG. 7.9.   Trend analysis of a repeated measure in a two factor mixed design.

   If more than one repeated measures factor is to be tested, it is initiated
through a second CONTRAST subcommand, as seen in Fig. 7.11. A single
RENAME subcommand can suffice for both. Given two repeated measures
within a mixed design, and trend tests on both, the tests for interactions
between the repeated measures trends will be found in the printout, as
previously described for designs in which only repeated measures are present.

Trend Tests on Between Subjects Factors in Mixed Designs

Assume a mixed design that includes a request for the standard analysis
of variance F tests. A request for a trend test on a between subjects factor
must *follow* the first DESIGN subcommand, as illustrated, for a two factor
mixed design, in Fig. 7.12. Note that, in Fig. 7.12, the SIGNIF(UNIV)
specification in the PRINT subcommand is omitted. It is recommended

```
TITLE THREE FACTORS, TWO REPEATED MEASURES (B & C)
SUBTITLE TREND TEST ON ONE REPEATED MEASURE (C)
DATA LIST LIST/A B1C1 B1C2 B1C3 B2C1 B2C2 B2C3
MANOVA B1C1 B1C2 B1C3 B2C1 B2C2 B2C3 BY A(1,3)
   /WSFACTORS = B(2) C(3)
   /CONTRAST(C) = POLYNOMIAL
   /RENAME = MEAN B LC QC BXLC BXQC
   /PRINT = CELLINFO(MEANS) SIGNIF(UNIV)
   /DESIGN
BEGIN DATA
   .
   .
   .
```

FIG. 7.10.   Trend tests on one of two repeated measures in a mixed three factor
design.

```
TITLE THREE FACTORS, TWO REPEATED MEASURES (B & C)
SUBTITLE TREND TESTS ON BOTH OF THE REPEATED MEASURES
DATA LIST LIST/A B1C1 B1C2 B1C3 B2C1 B2C2 B2C3 B3C1
  B3C2 B3C3
MANOVA B1C1 B1C2 B1C3 B2C1 B2C2 B2C3 B3C1 B3C2 B3C3 BY A(1,3)
   /WSFACTORS = B(3) C(3)
   /CONTRAST(B) = POLYNOMIAL
   /CONTRAST(C) = POLYNOMIAL
   /RENAME = MEAN LB QB LC QC LBXLC LBXQC QBXLC QBXQC
   /PRINT = CELLINFO(MEANS) SIGNIF(UNIV)
   /DESIGN
BEGIN DATA
   .
   .
   .
```

FIG. 7.11.   Trend tests on the two repeated measures in a mixed three factor design.

```
TITLE TWO FACTOR MIXED DESIGN, ONE REPEATED MEASURE C, TREND OF A
DATA LIST LIST/A C1 C2 C3 C4
MANOVA C1 C2 C3 C4 BY A(1,3)
   /WSFACTORS = C(4)
   /PRINT = CELLINFO(MEANS)
   /DESIGN
   /CONTRAST(A) = POLYNOMIAL
   /DESIGN = A(1) A(2)
BEGIN DATA
   .
   .
   .
```

FIG. 7.12.   Trend analysis on a between subjects factor in a two factor mixed design.

that it be omitted when the only trend request is for a between subjects factor. Under those circumstances the presence of SIGNIF(UNIV) adds some univariate test tables that can be confusing. However, when a trend of a repeated measures factor is included, the SIGNIF(UNIV) specification is necessary for producing the trend tests of the repeated measures in the printout.

With additional between subjects factors the program in Fig. 7.12 would be essentially the same, with the exception of the DATA LIST and MANOVA commands, which would include the specifications of the additional between subjects factors, as illustrated in Fig. 7.13, where it is assumed that an additional between subjects factor, B, has just two levels.

For interactions between trend tests for two between subjects factors, both of which are contained within a mixed design, the specific interactions have to be requested. The procedures for interactions among between subjects trend tests are the same in the context of mixed designs as in completely randomized designs, which are detailed in a preceding section titled Interactions of Trend Tests for Between Subjects Factors.

```
TITLE THREE FACTOR MIXED DESIGN, WITH REPEATED MEASURE C
SUBTITLE TREND ANALYSIS ON FACTOR A
DATA LIST LIST/A B C1 C2 C3 C4
MANOVA C1 C2 C3 C4 BY A(1,3) B(1,2)
   /WSFACTORS = C(4)
   /PRINT = CELLINFO(MEANS)
   /DESIGN
   /CONTRAST(A) = POLYNOMIAL
   /DESIGN = A(1) A(2)
BEGIN DATA
   .
   .
   .
```

FIG. 7.13.   Trend analysis on a between subjects factor in a three factor mixed design.

Trend Tests on Both Between and Within Subjects Factors

If trend analyses are to be requested on both a repeated measures factor and a between subjects factor in the same design, the repeated measures trend analysis is placed first, followed by a request for a full analysis (of the omnibus and interaction F tests), followed by a request for a trend analysis on the between subjects factor. This is illustrated in both Figs. 7.14 and 7.15, which, respectively, contain programs for a two and a three factor design.

Interactions between the trends of mixed factors are automatically computed. Illustrations of that information's appearance within the printouts are found near the end of this chapter, in the section on reading the printouts.

```
TITLE TWO FACTOR MIXED DESIGN, WITH REPEATED MEASURE C
SUBTITLE TREND ANALYSIS ON BOTH FACTORS
DATA LIST LIST/A C1 C2 C3
MANOVA C1 C2 C3 BY A(1,3)
   /WSFACTORS=C(3)
   /CONTRAST(C)=POLYNOMIAL
   /RENAME=MEAN LINEAR QUADR
   /PRINT=CELLINFO(MEANS) SIGNIF(UNIV)
   /DESIGN
   /CONTRAST(A)=POLYNOMIAL
   /DESIGN=A(1) A(2)
BEGIN DATA
   .
   .
   .
```

FIG. 7.14.   Trend analysis on both factors in a two factor mixed design.

```
TITLE THREE FACTOR MIXED DESIGN, WITH REPEATED MEASURE C
SUBTITLE TREND ANALYSIS ON FACTORS A AND C
DATA LIST LIST/A B C1 C2 C3
MANOVA C1 C2 C3 BY A(1,3) B(1,3)
   /WSFACTORS=C(3)
   /CONTRAST(C)=POLYNOMIAL
   /RENAME=MEAN LINEAR QUADR
   /PRINT=CELLINFO(MEANS) SIGNIF(UNIV)
   /DESIGN
   /CONTRAST(A)=POLYNOMIAL
   /DESIGN=A(1) A(2)
BEGIN DATA
   .
   .
   .
```

FIG. 7.15.   Trend analysis on factors A and C in a three factor mixed design.

Extrapolation to Designs with Additional Factors

Figures 7.14 and 7.15 should serve to illustrate how additional between subjects factors are accommodated. They are merely specified in the DATA LIST and MANOVA command lines. The same is true of additional repeated measures factors, with the added complication of combining the levels. If trends on more than one between subjects factor are desired, Fig. 7.4 indicates the manner in which a trend analysis on a second between subjects factor is requested in a completely randomized design. The same approach is used for mixed designs. Figure 7.7 illustrates a multiple contrast request in a repeated measures design, and this same approach is used for multiple repeated measures trends in a mixed design. The differences in requests for interactions of between subjects trends and repeated measures trends that were discussed previously remain true for mixed designs. If the trend factors are themselves mixed, all the interactions are given without special requests, as long as the univariate tests are requested in the PRINT subcommand with PRINT = SIGNIF(UNIV).

SIMPLE EFFECTS OF TRENDS

There are two kinds of trend interactions of interest, the interaction of a trend with another factor, and the interaction of two trends. When a test of an interaction of a trend with another factor is found to be statistically significant, it suggests that a particular trend, say a linear trend, is different at different levels of the second factor. It is possible, in this case, that a trend on factor A is statistically significant at one level of factor B, but not at another. Therefore, when the interaction of a trend with another factor is found significant, it is important to do simple trend tests; that is, tests of the trend of factor A, at each of the levels of factor B, to see where

```
TITLE TWO BET. SUBJ. FACTORS, SIMPLE EFFECTS OF A TREND
DATA LIST LIST/A B SCORE
MANOVA SCORE BY A(1,3) B(1,3)
  /CONTRASTS(A) = POLYNOMIAL
  /PRINT = CELLINFO(MEANS)
  /DESIGN = A(1) A(2) A(1) BY B
  /DESIGN = A(1) WITHIN B(1) A(1) WITHIN B(2) A(1) WITHIN B(3)
  /DESIGN
BEGIN DATA
    .
    .
    .
```

FIG. 7.16. Program for obtaining trends of factor A, the interaction of the linear trend of factor A with a second factor, and the simple effects of the linear trend, in a two factor completely randomized design. A third DESIGN subcommand is added to yield a full analysis.

statistical significance for the trend exists. Figure 7.16 offers a program for a two factor completely randomized design, where one set of trend tests (on factor A) are requested, along with a test of the interaction of the linear trend test of A with factor B, plus a test of the simple effects of the linear trend of A.

In Fig. 7.16, the first DESIGN subcommand, by including the specifi-

```
TITLE TWO FACTOR REPEATED MEASURES, SIMPLE EFFECTS OF A TREND
DATA LIST LIST/B1C1 B1C2 B1C3 B2C1 B2C2 B2C3
 B3C1 B3C2 B3C3
MANOVA B1C1 B1C2 B1C3 B2C1 B2C2 B2C3 B3C1 B3C2 B3C3
  /WSFACTORS=B(3) C(3)
  /CONTRAST(B)=POLYNOMIAL
  /CONTRAST(C)=POLYNOMIAL
  /RENAME=MEAN LB QB LC QC LBXLC LBXQC QBXLC QBXQC
  /PRINT=CELLINFO(MEANS) SIGNIF(UNIV)
  /WSDESIGN
  /DESIGN
  /WSDESIGN=B(1) BY C
  /DESIGN
  /WSDESIGN=B WITHIN C(1) B WITHIN C(2) B WITHIN C(3)
  /DESIGN
BEGIN DATA
 .
 .
 .
```

FIG. 7.17. Program for obtaining trends, the interaction of a linear trend of one factor with a second factor, and the simple effects of the linear trend, in a two factor repeated measures design.

```
TITLE TWO FACTOR MIXED, TRENDS AND SIMPLE EFFECTS ON A
DATA LIST LIST/A C1 C2 C3
MANOVA C1 C2 C3 BY A(1,3)
  /WSFACTORS=C(3)
  /CONTRAST(C)=POLYNOMIAL
  /RENAME=MEAN LINEAR QUADR
  /PRINT=CELLINFO(MEANS) SIGNIF(UNIV)
  /WSDESIGN
  /DESIGN
  /CONTRAST(A)=POLYNOMIAL
  /DESIGN=A(1) A(2)
  /WSDESIGN=MWITHIN C(1) MWITHIN C(2) MWITHIN C(3)
  /DESIGN=A(1) A(2)
BEGIN DATA
 .
 .
 .
```

FIG. 7.18. Trends and simple effects on the between subjects factor A in a two factor mixed design. The first CONTRAST subcommand and its immediately following RENAME subcommand are not strictly necessary. The SPSS program automatically tests the within subjects factor (C in this example) for trends when there is a request for a trend analysis on a between subjects factor in a mixed design, and then includes the interactions of the trends in the printouts. It is helpful, given these analyses, to include the RENAME subcommand because the different tests are than more clearly labeled.

cation A(1) BY B, requests the test of the interaction of the linear trend of A with factor B. The second DESIGN subcommand contains the specifications for the simple effects tests of the linear trends of A.

Figure 7.17 offers a program for a two factor repeated measures design, which includes requests for simple effects of a linear trend.

In Fig. 7.17 trend tests are requested on both factors. A test of the interaction of the linear trend of B with factor C is also requested, with the specification B(1) BY C in the second WSDESIGN subcommand. The simple effects of the linear trend of B are requested within the third WSDESIGN subcommand. Note that, with repeated measures, the simple effects tests for trends should not specify the specific trends, this is only done with between subjects factors, as seen in Fig. 7.16. That is, with repeated measures, one would not ask for B(1) WITHIN C(1), but rather for B WITHIN C(1), as seen in Fig. 7.17.

The inclusion in Fig. 7.17 of the second WSDESIGN subcommand and its specification B(1) BY C, plus its immediately following DESIGN subcommand, can be omitted from the program; the program would still run the simple effects tests. These two subcommands are included because simple effects tests such as the one requested in Fig. 7.17 are usually only justified by a statistically significant interaction.

Figures 7.18 and 7.19 also offer examples of programs combining trends and simple effects tests, but for mixed designs.

The program in Fig. 7.18 includes tests of the trends of the between subjects factor (A), each of which is restricted to a specific level of the repeated measures factor (C). The program in Fig. 7.19 includes tests of the trends of the repeated measures factor C, each of which is restricted to a specific level of the between subjects factor (A). The programs in Figs. 7.18 and 7.19 have been written so that full analyses will be produced.

```
TITLE TWO FACTOR MIXED, TRENDS AND SIMPLE EFFECTS ON C
DATA LIST LIST/A C1 C2 C3
MANOVA C1 C2 C3 BY A(1,3)
  /WSFACTORS = C(3)
  /CONTRASTS(C) = POLYNOMIAL
  /RENAME = MEAN LINEAR QUADR
  /PRINT = CELLINFO(MEANS) SIGNIF(UNIV)
  /WSDESIGN
  /DESIGN
  /WSDESIGN = C
  /DESIGN = MWITHIN A(1) MWITHIN A(2) MWITHIN A(3)
BEGIN DATA
  .
  .
  .
```

FIG. 7.19. Trends and simple effects on the repeated measures of factor C in a two factor mixed design.

For example, the program in Fig. 7.19 will yield the main effect trends of C, as well as the specified simple effects.

If a trend test were desired on the between subjects factor A as well as the repeated measures factor C, in Fig. 7.19, CONTRAST and DESIGN subcommands would follow the last DESIGN subcommand that contains the MWITHIN keywords. Specifically,

```
TITLE THREE FACTORS, TWO REPEATED MEASURES (B & C)
SUTITLE SIMPLE INTERACTION OF TRENDS ON A & C
DATA LIST LIST/A B1C1 B1C2 B1C3 B2C1 B2C2 B2C3 B3C1
 B3C2 B3C3
MANOVA B1C1 B1C2 B1C3 B2C1 B2C2 B2C3 B3C1 B3C2 B3C3 BY A(1,3)
  /WSFACTORS=B(3) C(3)
  /CONTRAST(B)=POLYNOMIAL
  /CONTRAST(C)=POLYNOMIAL
  /RENAME=MEAN LB QB LC QC LBXLC LBXQC QBXLC QBXQC
  /PRINT=CELLINFO(MEANS) SIGNIF(UNIV)
  /WSDESIGN
  /DESIGN
  /WSDESIGN=C WITHIN B(1) C WITHIN B(2)
  /DESIGN
  /CONTRAST(A)=POLYNOMIAL
  /DESIGN=A(1) A(2)
BEGIN DATA
  .
  .
  .
```

FIG. 7.20.   Simple interaction of trends on mixed factors (A and C) at selected levels of a repeated measures factor (B), in a three factor mixed design. The request for a set of trends on factor B is optional; the program would yield the desired simple interaction of trends without it.

```
TITLE THREE FACTORS, TWO REPEATED MEASURES (B & C)
SUBTITLE SIMPLE INTERACTION OF TRENDS ON B & C
DATA LIST LIST/A B1C1 B1C2 B1C3 B2C1 B2C2 B2C3 B3C1
 B3C2 B3C3
MANOVA B1C1 B1C2 B1C3 B2C1 B2C2 B2C3 B3C1 B3C2 B3C3 BY A(1,3)
  /WSFACTORS=B(3) C(3)
  /CONTRAST(B)=POLYNOMIAL
  /CONTRAST(C)=POLYNOMIAL
  /RENAME=MEAN LB QB LC QC LBXLC LBXQC QBXLC QBXQC
  /PRINT=CELLINFO(MEANS) SIGNIF(UNIV)
  /WSDESIGN
  /DESIGN
  /WSDESIGN=C BY B
  /DESIGN=MWITHIN A(1) MWITHIN A(2)
BEGIN DATA
  .
  .
  .
```

FIG. 7.21.   Simple interaction of trends on repeated measures factors (B and C) at selected levels of between subjects factor (A), in a three factor mixed design.

```
/CONTRAST(A)=POLYNOMIAL
/DESIGN=A(1) A(2)
```

would appear just prior to the BEGIN DATA command.

Simple Effects of Interactions Between Trends

When working with a three factor design, simple effects of an interaction between trends can be of interest. For example, in a three factor mixed design with two repeated measures, there could be interest in the interaction between the trends on one repeated measure (C) and the between subjects factor (A), at a specific level of factor B. Figure 7.20 offers an example of a program that would yield this simple interaction of trends.

If what was desired, was the interaction of the two repeated measures trends (B and C) at selected levels of the between subjects factor A, Fig. 7.21 would offer an appropriate program, assuming the same three factor mixed design.

In Fig. 7.21, the critical component for obtaining the simple effect of the interaction of two repeated measures trends, is specifying, in the second WSDESIGN subcommand, that the interaction is to be reanalyzed, but as a simple effects test as specified in the second DESIGN subcommand.

For a three factor design with only one repeated measures factor (C), one might wish to look at the simple interaction of the two between subjects factors trends, at one level of the repeated measures factor. An appropriate program is shown in Fig. 7.22.

It is critical, in Fig. 7.22, that the specific interaction between the two between subject factor trends that are desired be specified, as with A(1) BY B(2), along with the level of the third factor at which the simple effect is to be tested, as in MWITHIN C(1).

```
TITLE THREE FACTORS, ONE REPEATED MEASURE, C
SUBTITLE SIMPLE INTERACTION OF TRENDS ON A & B
DATA LIST LIST/A B C1 C2 C3 C4
MANOVA C1 C2 C3 C4 BY A(1,3) B(1,3)
  /WSFACTORS=C(4)
  /PRINT=CELLINFO(MEANS) SIGNIF(UNIV)
  /WSDESIGN
  /DESIGN
  /CONTRAST(A)=POLYNOMIAL
  /CONTRAST(B)=POLYNOMIAL
  /WSDESIGN=MWITHIN C(1)
  /DESIGN=A(1) A(2) B(1) B(2) A(1) BY B(2)
BEGIN DATA
  .
  .
  .
```

FIG. 7.22.   Simple interaction of trends on between subjects factors A and B at the first level of repeated measures factor C, in a three factor mixed design.

```
TITLE THREE FACTORS, ONE REPEATED MEASURE, C
SUBTITLE SIMPLE INTERACTION OF TRENDS ON A & C
DATA LIST LIST/A B C1 C2 C3 C4
MANOVA C1 C2 C3 C4 BY A(1,3) B(1,3)
  /WSFACTORS = C(4)
  /CONTRAST(C) = POLYNOMIAL
  /RENAME = MEAN LINEAR QUADR CUBIC
  /PRINT = CELLINFO(MEANS) SIGNIF(UNIV)
  /WSDESIGN
  /DESIGN
  /CONTRAST(A) = POLYNOMIAL
  /DESIGN = A(1) A(2)
  /DESIGN = A(1) WITHIN B(1) A(1) WITHIN B(2) A(2) WITHIN B(1)
    A(2) WITHIN B(2)
BEGIN DATA
   .
   .
   .
```

FIG. 7.23. Simple interaction of trends on between subjects factor A and repeated measures factor C, at levels one and two of between subjects factor B, in a three factor mixed design.

Still assuming the design used in Fig. 7.22, that is, three factors with one repeated measures factor C, the interest could be in a simple trend interaction of factors A and C. Specifically, assume that the interaction of the trends of factors A and C is to be examined at the first two levels of factor B. Figure 7.23 gives the correct program for this purpose, which also includes the main effects analysis.

SIMPLE SIMPLE EFFECTS OF TRENDS

In a three factor design, simple simple trends can be needed. For example, in a three factor design with one repeated measure C, one might wish to

```
TITLE THREE FACTORS, ONE REPEATED MEASURE, C
SUBTITLE SIMPLE SIMPLE TRENDS OF C
DATA LIST LIST/A B C1 C2 C3 C4
MANOVA C1 C2 C3 C4 BY A(1,3) B(1,3)
  /WSFACTORS = C(4)
  /CONTRAST(C) = POLYNOMIAL
  /RENAME = MEAN LINEAR QUADRA
  /PRINT = CELLINFO(MEANS) SIGNIF(UNIV)
  /WSDESIGN
  /DESIGN
  /WSDESIGN = C
  /DESIGN = MWITHIN A(1) WITHIN B(1) MWITHIN A(1) WITHIN B(2)
BEGIN DATA
   .
   .
   .
```

FIG. 7.24. Simple simple trends on the one repeated measure, C, at specified levels of A and B, in a three factor design.

```
TITLE THREE FACTORS, ONE REPEATED MEASURE, C
SUBTITLE SIMPLE SIMPLE TREND OF B
DATA LIST LIST/A B C1 C2 C3 C4
MANOVA C1 C2 C3 C4 BY A(1,3) B(1,3)
   /WSFACTORS = C(4)
   /PRINT = CELLINFO(MEANS) SIGNIF(UNIV)
   /WSDESIGN
   /DESIGN
   /CONTRAST(B) = POLYNOMIAL
   /DESIGN = B(1) B(2)
   /WSDESIGN = MWITHIN C(1) MWITHIN C(2) MWITHIN C(3) MWITHIN C(4)
   /DESIGN = B(1) WITHIN A(1) B(2) WITHIN A(1)
BEGIN DATA
   .
   .
   .
```

FIG. 7.25. Simple simple trends on one of the between subjects factors, B, restricted to the first level of A, examined within each of the levels of C, which is the single repeated measure in a three factor design.

```
TITLE THREE FACTORS, TWO REPEATED MEASURES B AND C
SUBTITLE SIMPLE SIMPLE TRENDS OF A
DATA LIST LIST/A B1C1 B1C2 B1C3 B2C1 B2C2 B2C3 B3C1
 B3C2 B3C3
MANOVA B1C1 B1C2 B1C3 B2C1 B2C2 B2C3 B3C1 B3C2 B3C3 BY A(1,3)
   /WSFACTORS = B(3) C(3)
   /PRINT = CELLINFO(MEANS) SIGNIF(UNIV)
   /WSDESIGN
   /DESIGN
   /CONTRAST(A) = POLYNOMIAL
   /DESIGN = A(1) A(2)
   /WSDESIGN = MWITHIN C(1) WITHIN B(1) MWITHIN C(1) WITHIN B(2)
   /DESIGN = A(1)
BEGIN DATA
   .
   .
   .
```

FIG. 7.26. Simple simple trends on the between subjects factor A, in a three factor design with two repeated measures (B and C). The linear trend of A is tested at the first level of C within the first two levels of factor B.

test the trends of C at the first level of A within both the first and second levels of B. Figure 7.24 offers a program that would yield such a test.

Assume that, for the same design (three factors, one of which, C, is a repeated measure), what is desired is the following simple simple trend: each of the trends on factor B, restricted to the first level of A, examined within each of the levels of C. Figure 7.25 offers an appropriate program.

As another example, assume a three factor design with two repeated measures, B and C. Assume that the interest is in the linear trend of A restricted to the first level of C, examined at the first two levels of B. Figure 7.26 gives a program that would yield these tests.

Assume the same design again, that is, a three factor design with two repeated measures, B and C. Assume that the interest this time is in the trends of C restricted to the first level of A, within each of the two levels of B. Figure 7.27 gives a program that would yield these results.

COMBINING TRENDS AND CONTRASTS

Interactions of contrasts were illustrated in the preceding chapter, and interactions of trends have been illustrated in this chapter. Because of the similarity between contrasts and trends, it is a simple matter to combine trends and contrasts for, say, a contrasts of trends, in the same way as for

```
TITLE THREE FACTOR DESIGN WITH TWO REPEATED MEASURES, B & C
SUBTITLE SIMPLE SIMPLE TRENDS OF C
DATA LIST LIST/A B1C1 B1C2 B1C3 B2C1 B2C2 B2C3
 B3C1 B3C2 B3C3
MANOVA B1C1 B1C2 B1C3 B2C1 B2C2 B2C3 B3C1 B3C2 B3C3 BY A(1,3)
   /WSFACTORS=B(3) C(3)
   /CONTRAST(C)=POLYNOMIAL
   /RENAME=MEAN LB QB LC QC LBXLC LBXQC QBXLC QBXQC
   /PRINT-CELLINFO(MEANS) SIGNIF(UNIV)
   /WSDESIGN
   /DESIGN
   /WSDESIGN=C WITHIN B(1) C WITHIN B(2)
   /DESIGN=MWITHIN A(1)
BEGIN DATA
  .
  .
  .
```

FIG. 7.27.   Simple simple trends on one of two repeated measures (C), in a three factor design. The trends of C are tested at the first level of A within the first and second levels of B.

```
TITLE THREE FACTOR MIXED DESIGN, WITH REPEATED MEASURE C
SUBTITLE TREND AND CONTRAST INTERACTION, TREND A, CONTRAST B
DATA LIST LIST/A B C1 C2 C3 C4
MANOVA C1 C2 C3 C4 BY A(1,3) B(1,3)
   /WSFACTORS=C(4)
   /PRINT=CELLINFO(MEANS) SIGNIF(UNIV)
   /DESIGN
   /CONTRAST(A)=POLYNOMIAL
   /CONTRAST(B)=SPECIAL(3*1, 0,-1,1, 2,-1,-1)
   /DESIGN=A(1) A(2) B(1) B(2) A(1) BY B(1) A(1) BY B(2)
BEGIN DATA
  .
  .
  .
```

FIG. 7.28.   Trend and contrast interaction in a three factor design with one repeated measure (C). The trend test is on factor A, and the contrast is on factor B. The A(1) in the second design subcommand represents the linear trend of A, A(2) the quadratic trend, while B(1) and B(2) are the two contrasts on B.

an interaction of contrasts, or an interaction of trends. That is, the program could contain a CONTRAST request on one factor for a trend, and a CONTRAST request on another factor for a specific (SPECIAL) contrast. The test of the interaction of the trend and the special contrast is a test of a contrast of trends.

For example, assume a three factor design, with three levels for each factor, and a linear trend test on factor A. One might have hypothesized that the linear trend on factor A, the slope, is higher at level three than level two of factor B. This would be tested through a test of the interaction of the linear trend of A and a contrast on B with the weights $0, -1, 1$. Further, one might also hypothesize that the slope for factor A is highest at the first level of B, that is, higher at the first level of B than at both of the other levels of B. This would be tested as an interaction of the linear trend of A with a contrast on B that has the weights $2, -1, -1$.

The specific SPSS-X program statements for such trend and contrast interactions would vary with which factors were repeated measures and which were between subjects factors. The many preceding figures should offer a good guide to the possibilities for varied combinations, merely substituting CONTRASTS( ) = SPECIAL subcommands for some of the CONTRAST( ) = POLYNOMIAL subcommands used in the earlier figures illustrating interactions. Some examples of trend by contrast interactions are provided in Figs. 7.28 through 7.30. Figure 7.28 examines the interaction of a trend on A and a contrast on B, where both are between subjects factors in a three factor mixed design.

Figure 7.29 examines the interaction of a trend on between subjects

```
TITLE THREE FACTORS, TWO REPEATED MEASURES (B & C)
SUBTITLE TREND & CONTRAST INTERACTION, TREND A, CONTRAST B
DATA LIST LIST/A B1C1 B1C2 B1C3 B2C1 B2C2 B2C3 B3C1
  B3C2 B3C3
MANOVA B1C1 B1C2 B1C3 B2C1 B2C2 B2C3 B3C1 B3C2 B3C3 BY A(1,3)
   /WSFACTORS=B(3) C(3)
   /CONTRAST(B)=SPECIAL(3*1, 0,-1,1, 2,-1,-1)
   /RENAME=MEAN B1 B2 C1 C2 B1XC1 B1XC2 B2XC1 B2XC2
   /PRINT=CELLINFO(MEANS) SIGNIF(UNIV)
   /DESIGN
   /CONTRAST(A)=POLYNOMIAL
   /DESIGN=A(1) A(2)
BEGIN DATA
  .
  .
  .
```

FIG. 7.29.   Trend and contrast interaction, in a three factor design with two repeated measures (B and C). The trend test is on factor A, and the contrast is on factor B. Because the interaction includes both a repeated measure and a between subjects factor, the interaction tests do not have to be specified as in Fig. 7.28; they are automatically included in the printout.

```
TITLE TWO FACTORS, REPEATED MEASURES B & C
TREND (B) AND CONTRAST (C) INTERACTIONS
DATA LIST LIST/B1C1 B1C2 B1C3 B2C1 B2C2 B2C3 B3C1
 B3C2 B3C3
MANOVA B1C1 B1C2 B1C3 B2C1 B2C2 B2C3 B3C1 B3C2 B3C3
  /WSFACTORS=B(3) C(3)
  /CONTRAST(B)=POLYNOMIAL
  /CONTRAST(C)=SPECIAL (3*1, 0,-1,1, 2,-1,-1)
  /RENAME=MEAN LB QB C1 C2 LBXC1 LBXC2 QBXC1 QBXC2
  /PRINT=CELLINFO(MEANS) SIGNIF(UNIV)
  /DESIGN
BEGIN DATA
 .
 .
 .
```

FIG. 7.30.   Test of a trend and contrast interaction in a two factor repeated measures design. Note the names in the RENAME subcommand. The last four names label the specific trend and contrast interactions that are automatically provided in the printout. The sixth and seventh names, LBXC1 and LBXC2 will identify the rows containing the desired F tests for the interactions of the linear trend of B with the first and second contrasts on C.

```
TITLE THREE FACTOR MIXED DESIGN, WITH REPEATED MEASURE C
SUBTITLE TREND (A) AND CONTRAST (B) INTERACTION, AT C(1)
DATA LIST LIST/A B C1 C2 C3 C4
MANOVA C1 C2 C3 C4 BY A(1,3) B(1,3)
  /WSFACTORS=C(4)
  /PRINT=CELLINFO(MEANS) SIGNIF(UNIV)
  /WSDESIGN
  /DESIGN
  /CONTRAST(A)=POLYNOMIAL
  /CONTRAST(B)=SPECIAL(3*1, 2,-1,-1, 0,-1,1)
  /DESIGN=A(1) A(2) B(1) B(2) A(1) BY B(1) A(1) BY B(2)
  /WSDESIGN=MWITHIN C(1)
  /DESIGN=A(1) A(2) B(1) B(2) A(1) BY B(1) A(1) BY B(2)
BEGIN DATA
 .
 .
 .
```

FIG. 7.31.   Trend and contrast interaction in a three factor design with one repeated measure (C). The trend test is on factor A, and the contrast is on factor B, both between subjects factors. Also included is an analysis of the trends and interaction of trends and contrasts that are restricted to the first level of factor C, the repeated measure.

factor A and a contrast on repeated measures factor B, in a mixed design with two repeated measures (B and C).

Figure 7.30 offers an example of trend and contrast interactions where both the trend and contrast requests are on repeated measures, in this case in a two factor repeated measures design.

Figure 7.30 involves a two factor repeated measures design. If there were a third factor, say a between subjects factor A, it would merely be mentioned in the DATA LIST and MANOVA commands. The difference with the addition of a between subjects factor is therefore slight, and can be seen in a comparison of Figs. 7.7 and 7.11 of this chapter.

COMBINING TRENDS, CONTRASTS, AND SIMPLE EFFECTS

Since trends are merely particular contrasts, the illustrations in the prior section titled Simple Effects of Interactions Between Trends, can be used when combining trends, contrasts, and simple effects. However, specific examples are again offered here, where one of the trends is a special contrast.

As the first example, assume a three factor design with two between subject factors, A and B, and a repeated measures factor C. One could ask whether the linear trend of A, symbolized as A(1), is different at the second and third levels of factor B, this contrast being symbolized by B(2), but restricting the analysis to the first level of repeated measures factor C. This is illustrated in Fig. 7.31

In the same basic design as that used in Fig. 7.31, one could ask about the simple effect of the contrast of a trend, where the contrast is on between subjects factor (B), but the trend is one the repeated measures factor (C). Assume that the question is whether the trends are different on factor C, when comparing them at levels two and three of factor B, but with the question restricted to the first level of factor A. This is illustrated in Fig. 7.32.

Figure 7.33 offers a simple effects analysis of a mixed trend and contrast interaction (B and A, respectively), for a three factor design with two repeated measures (B and C), with the simple effects of the contrast of a trend examined at each level of factor C.

```
TITLE THREE FACTORS, ONE REPEATED MEASURE, C,
SUBTITLE CONTRAST ON B OF TRENDS OF C, AT LEVEL ONE OF A
DATA LIST LIST/A B C1 C2 C3 C4
MANOVA C1 C2 C3 C4 BY A(1,3) B(1,3)
   /WSFACTORS = C(4)
   /CONTRAST(C) = POLYNOMIAL
   /RENAME = MEAN LINEAR QUADR CUBIC
   /PRINT = CELLINFO(MEANS) SIGNIF(UNIV)
   /DESIGN
   /CONTRAST(B) = SPECIAL(3*1, 0,1,-1, 2,-1,1)
   /DESIGN = B(1) B(2)
   /DESIGN = B(1) WITHIN A(1)
BEGIN DATA
   .
   .
   .
```

FIG. 7.32. Simple contrast of trends, testing whether the trends on repeated measures factor C are different at levels two and three of between subjects factor B, restricting the question to the first level of between subjects factor A.

```
TITLE THREE FACTORS, TWO REPEATED MEASURED (B & C)
SUBTITLE TREND (B) & CONTRAST (A) INTERACTION
DATA LIST LIST/A B1C1 B1C2 B1C3 B2C1 B2C2 B2C3 B3C1
  B3C2 B3C3
MANOVA B1C1 B1C2 B1C3 B2C1 B2C2 B2C3 B3C1 B3C2 B3C3 BY A(1,3)
  /WSFACTORS=B(3) C(3)
  /CONTRAST(B)=POLYNOMIAL
  /CONTRAST(C)=POLYNOMIAL
  /RENAME=MEAN LB QB LC QC LBXLC LBXQC QBXLC QBXQC
  /PRINT=CELLINFO(MEANS) SIGNIF(UNIV)
  /WSDESIGN
  /DESIGN
  /WSDESIGN=B WITHIN C(1) B WITHIN C(2) B WITHIN C(3)
  /DESIGN=A(1) A(2)
  /CONTRAST(A)=SPECIAL(3*1, -1,1,0, 1,1,-2)
  /DESIGN=A(1) A(2)
BEGIN DATA
  .
  .
  .
```

FIG. 7.33.   Trend and contrast interaction, in a three factor design with two repeated measures (B and C). Trend tests on both B and C are requested, along with contrasts on factor A. Also included is a simple interaction analysis of the trend (of B) and contrast (of A), within levels of C.

```
TITLE THREE FACTORS, TWO REPEATED MEASURES (B & C)
SUBTITLE TREND (B), CONTRAST (C) INTERACTION, AT A(1)
DATA LIST LIST/A B1C1 B1C2 B1C3 B2C1 B2C2 B2C3 B3C1
  B3C2 B3C3
MANOVA B1C1 B1C2 B1C3 B2C1 B2C2 B2C3 B3C1 B3C2 B3C3 BY A(1,3)
  /WSFACTORS=B(3) C(3)
  /CONTRAST(B)=POLYNOMIAL
  /CONTRAST(C)=SPECIAL(3*1, 2,-1,-1, 0,-1,1)
  /RENAME=MEAN LB QB C1 C2 LBXC1 LBXC2 QBXC1 QBXC2
  /PRINT=CELLINFO(MEANS) SIGNIF(UNIV)
  /WSDESIGN
  /DESIGN
  /WSDESIGN=B BY C
  /DESIGN=MWITHIN A(1)
BEGIN DATA
  .
  .
  .
```

FIG. 7.34.   Trend and contrast interaction, in a three factor design with two repeated measures (B and C). The trend test is on B, and the contrast is on factor C, and includes the analysis restricted to the first level of factor A.

In Fig. 7.33, the request for simple effects in the second WSDESIGN subcommand must follow, as it does, the DESIGN subcommand associated with the main effect trend requests. It must also precede the contrast requests on the between subjects factor, in order to obtain simple effects for the mixed interaction.

Figure 7.34 offers a simple effects analysis of the trend and contrast

```
* * * * * * * * * * ANALYSIS OF VARIANCE -- DESIGN  1  * * *
```

TESTS OF SIGNIFICANCE FOR SCORE USING UNIQUE SUMS OF SQUARES

SOURCE OF VARIATION	SS	DF	MS	F	SIG OF F
WITHIN CELLS	14.80	12	1.23		
A(1)	8.10	1	8.10	6.57	.025
A(2)	2.70	1	2.70	2.19	.165

FIG. 7.35. Illustrative printout table giving the trend tests for a between subjects factor. The word SCORE appears only if that is the label used for the dependent variable.

```
* * * * * * * * * * * ANALYSIS OF VARIANCE -- DESIGN  1  * * *
```

TESTS OF SIGNIFICANCE FOR SCORE USING UNIQUE SUMS OF SQUARES

SOURCE OF VARIATION	SS	DF	MS	F	SIG OF F
WITHIN CELLS	74.83	45	1.66		
A(1)	3.36	1	3.36	2.02	.162
A(2)	17.12	1	17.12	10.30	.002
B(1)	380.25	1	380.25	228.66	.000
B(2)	412.23	1	412.23	247.89	.000
A(1) BY B	187.72	2	93.86	56.44	.000
A(1) BY B(1)	1.13	1	1.13	.68	.415

FIG. 7.36. Trend tests on both factors, test of an interaction of the linear trend of A and factor B, and test of the linear by linear interaction of factors A and B, in a two factor completely randomized design.

interaction of the two repeated measures (B and C), within a three factor design, along with the full factorial analysis of these interactions.

In Fig. 7.34, it is the B BY C specification within the second WSDESIGN subcommand, along with the specification MWITHIN A(1) in the second DESIGN subcommand, that yields the simple effects analysis of the desired interactions.

THE PRINTOUTS FOR TREND ANALYSES

The printouts for trend analyses are discussed in five separate sections; Completely Randomized Designs, Repeated Measures Designs, Mixed Designs, Simple Trends, and Simple Simple Trends.

Completely Randomized Designs

The tests for trends of between subjects factors will always appear in similar tables, regardless of whether the design is a completely randomized or mixed design. Figure 7.35 offers an illustration of the trend tests in a one factor completely randomized design.

The specific trend tests appear in the order, LINEAR, QUADRATIC,

CUBIC, etc., but are not labeled that way. Instead, they are labeled A(1), A(2), A(3), etc., if the factor is named A; or FACTOR(1), FACTOR(2), etc., if it is named FACTOR (since that is what would have appeared as the specification in the DESIGN subcommand). The error term appears in the line labeled WITHIN CELLS.

Figure 7.36 offers an illustration of the trend tests on two different factors, and a test of the interaction of the linear trend of A with factor B, and the linear by linear interaction of factors A and B, in a two factor completely randomized design.

```
EFFECT-C. (CONT.)
UNIVARIATE F-TESTS WITH (1,3) D. F.

VARIABLE       HYPOTH. SS     ERROR SS    . . .             F    SIG. OF F

LINEAR          171.11250      .53750      . . .      955.04651        .000
QUADR            14.00000   176.00000      . . .       14.00000        .108
CUBIC             9.65223   198.76000      . . .        9.00000        .916
```

FIG. 7.37. Test of trends in a one factor repeated measures design. The factor (C) has four levels, permitting linear, quadratic, and cubic trends to be tested. The names LINEAR, QUADR, and CUBIC were used in the RENAME subcommand. The central portion of the table, giving the means squares, is not shown.

```
EFFECT .. B BY C (CONT.)
UNIVARIATE F-TESTS WITH (1,5) D. F.,

VARIABLE       HYPOTH. SS     ERROR SS    . . .             F    SIG. OF F

LBXLC           2.66667    18.33333       . . .         .72727        .433
LBXQC           1.38889     3.61111       . . .        1.92308        .224
QBXLC            .05556     3.27778       . . .         .08475        .783
QBXQC            .29630     7.03704       . . .         .21053        .666
```

FIG. 7.38.   The interaction of trends, in a two factor repeated measures design, where the two factors each have three levels. The names (LBXLC, LBXQC, etc.) are those given in the RENAME subcommand. If B is the most slowly changing factor, then the interactions, in the order given, would be linear A by linear B, linear A by quadratic C, quadratic B by linear C, and quadratic B by quadratic C. The central portion of the table, giving the mean squares, is not shown. Figure 7.7 in this chapter illustrates a program that would produce this table.

```
* * * * * * * * * * * * ANALYSIS OF VARIANCE -- DESIGN  2 * *
TESTS INVOLVING 'C(1) BY B' WITHIN-SUBJECT EFFECT

AVERAGED TESTS OF SIGNIF FOR MEAS. 1 USING UNIQUE SUMS OF SQUARES
SOURCE OF VARIATION         SS        DF        MS         F    SIG OF F
WITHIN CELLS              5.87         8       .73
C(1) BY B               123.47         2     61.73     84.18        .000
```

FIG. 7.39.   Test of significance for interaction of the linear trend of C with factor B, when both are repeated measures.

Repeated Measures Designs

In a repeated measures design the trend tests appear in a table with a heading EFFECT—C (assuming C to be the name of the factor), and a subheading UNIVARIATE F-TESTS WITH (__,__) D. F., where the degrees of freedom for the trend and for its error term are contained within the parentheses. This is illustrated in Fig. 7.37.

If there are two repeated measures, B and C, and both were tested for trends, the tests would appear in a table similar to the one seen in Fig. 7.37. Assume three levels in each factor, and that the program contained the following nine labels in the RENAME subcommand: MEAN LB QB LC QC LBXLC LBXQC QBXLC QBXQC. In this case, LB and QB would be the row labels for the trends on B. A separate table would give the trends for C, with the row labels LC and QC. The interaction of the trends, the linear A by linear B, the linear A by quadratic B, etc., would appear in a third table, like that seen in Fig. 7.38.

Figure 7.39 offers a table showing the interaction of a linear trend of a factor C, with a factor B. Note that this is not an interaction of two trends, but rather of a trend with a factor. This is for two repeated measures, so would have to be specifically requested in a WSDESIGN subcommand. The set of program statements for this was seen in Fig. 7.8.

Mixed Designs

In a mixed design the table for between subjects trends would look similar to those seen in Figs. 7.35 and 7.36, and for repeated measures trends would look similar to those presented in Figs. 7.37 and 7.38. However, with mixed designs, some interactions between trends can be in tables that look a little different. Figure 7.40 gives an example of an interaction between a linear trend of a between subjects factor, A, and the trends (both linear and quadratic) of a repeated measures factor (C), in a two factor mixed design.

```
EFFECT .. A(1) BY C (CONT.)
UINIVARIATE F-TESTS WITH (1,9) D. F.
```

VARIABLE	HYPOTH. SS	ERROR SS	. . .	F	SIG. OF F
LINEAR	7.52083	6.29167	. . .	10.78528	.010
QUADRA	1.56250	14.37500	. . .	.97826	.348

FIG. 7.40. Interaction of the linear and quadratic trends on repeated measures factor C, with the linear trend of between subjects factor A. The central portion of the table, giving the mean squares, is not shown. A(1) in the heading refers to the linear trend on factor A. Figure 7.14 in this chapter illustrates a program that would produce this table.

EFFECT .. A BY C (CONT.)
UNIVARIATE F-TESTS WITH (2,9) D. F.

VARIABLE	HYPOTH. SS	ERROR SS	. . .	F	SIG. OF F
LINEAR	8.08333	6.29167	. . .	5.78146	.024
QUADRA	5.08333	·14.37500	. . .	1.59130	.256

FIG. 7.41. Interaction of the trends on a repeated measures factor C, with the between subjects factor A, in a two factor mixed design. The names LINEAR and QUADRA were used in the RENAME subcommand. In the table, each test is a test of whether the particular trend of C is different at the different levels of factor A. The central portion of the table, giving the mean squares, is not shown.

* * * * * * * * * * * * ANALYSIS OF VARIANCE — DESIGN 2 * *
TESTS INVOLVING 'C' WITHIN-SUBJECT EFFECT

AVERAGED TESTS OF SIGNIF FOR C USING UNIQUE SUMS OF SQUARES

SOURCE OF VARIATION	SS	DF	MS	F	SIG OF F
WITHIN CELLS	20.67	18	1.15		
C	118.17	2	59.08	51.45	.000
A(1) BY C	9.08	2	4.54	3.96	.038
A(2) BY C	4.08	2	2.04	1.78	.197

FIG. 7.42. Test of significance for repeated measures factor C, and tests of whether the linear trend, A(1), and quadratic trend, A(2), of the between subjects factor A, interact with repeated measures factor C.

* * * * * * * * * * ANALYSIS OF VARIANCE — DESIGN 2 * * * * *
TESTS OF SIGNIFICANCE FOR SCORE USING UNIQUE SUMS OF SQUARES

SOURCE OF VARIATION	SS	DF	MS	F	SIG OF F
WITHIN CELLS	74.83	45	1.66		
A(1) WITHIN B(1)	3.00	1	3.00	1.80	.186
A(1) WITHIN B(2)	140.08	1	140.08	84.24	.000
A(1) WITHIN B(3)	48.00	1	48.00	24.86	.000

FIG. 7.43. Simple trends in a two factor completely randomized design. A(1) is the linear trend on factor A, and B(1), B(2), and B(3) are the levels of factor B at which the linear trend for A is being tested. A program that would produce such a table is seen in Fig. 7.16 of this chapter.

Figure 7.41 offers an illustration of a table for the interaction of the trends on a repeated measures factor C, with the between subjects factor A, in a two factor mixed design. (Note that this is not a test of an interaction between two trends, but two tests of interactions: an interaction of the linear trend of a repeated measures factor C with between subjects factor A; and the same question in regard to the quadratic trend of C. The questions are whether the individual trends of C are different at the different levels of A.)

The principle headings in Figs. 7.41 and 7.38 have a similar appearance, but do not refer to the same tests. In Fig. 7.41 the factors in the table heading, EFFECT .. A BY C, are mixed, and the row labels refer to the trends for the repeated measures factor. Each trend of the factor (C) is tested for its interaction with factor A. In Fig. 7.38, the factors in the table heading EFFECT .. B BY C, are both repeated measures, and the row labels refer to interactions between trends on the two factors.

Figure 7.42 offers a table of tests of whether the trends of the between subjects factor A interact with the repeated measures factor C, in a two factor mixed design.

```
EFFECT .. B WITHIN C(1) (CONT.)
UNIVARIATE F-TESTS WITH (1,4) D. F.
```

VARIABLE	HYPOTH. SS	ERROR SS	. . .	F	SIG OF F
LB	.40000	.60000	. . .	2.66667	.178
QB	13.33333	5.00000	. . .	10.66667	.031

FIG. 7.44. Table showing a test of the simple effects of the linear and quadratic trends on factor B, at the first level of factor C, in a design where both factors B and C are repeated measures. The labels for each row (LB and QB) are not necessarily the labels that would appear in the table. See the text for a further discussion of these row labels. A program that would produce such a table is seen in Fig. 7.17 of this chapter.

```
* * * * * * * * * * ANALYSIS OF VARIANCE -- DESIGN  3 * * * *
TESTS INVOLVING 'MWITHIN C(1) WITHIN-SUBJECT EFFECT.
```

SOURCE OF VARIATION	SS	DF	MS	F	SIG OF F
WITHIN CELLS	24.75	9	2.75		
MWITHIN C(1)	126.75	1	126.75	46.09	.000
A(1) BY MWITHIN C(1)	8.00	1	8.00	2.91	.122
A(2) BY MWITHIN C(1)	1.50	1	1.50	.55	.479

FIG. 7.45. Table showing tests of the simple effects of the linear and quadratic trends on factor A, at the first level of repeated measures factor C, in a two factor mixed design. The WITHIN CELLS row offers the error term. The numerators in the F ratios, and the F tests, are found in the rows A(1) BY MWITHIN C(1), AND A(2) BY MWITHIN C(1). The MWITHIN C(1) row can be ignored for this design. Separate tables would present the tests for the different levels of factor C. Figure 7.18 in this chapter offers a program that would produce this table.

```
EFFECT .. MWITHIN A(1) BY C (CONT.)
UNIVARIATE F-TESTS WITH (1,9) D. F.
```

VARIABLE	HYPOTH. SS	ERROR SS	. . .	F	SIG OF F
LINEAR	8.16667	6.29167	. . .	11.68212	.008
QUADRA	12.50000	14.37500	. . .	7.82609	.021

FIG. 7.46. Simple effects of the trends on repeated measures factor C in a two factor mixed design. In this table the two linear and quadratic trends are each tested within the first level of factor A. Separate tables give the tests at the different levels of factor A. MWITHIN is a keyword in SPSS which can be read as "within" for the mixed design case. Thus the table heading can be read as C WITHIN A(1), in a mixed design. Figure 7.19 in this chapter presents a program that would produce such a table.

EFFECT .. A(1) BY C WITHIN B(1) (CONT.)
UNIVARIATE F-TESTS WITH (1,6) D. F.

VARIABLE	HYPOTH. SS	ERROR SS	. . .	F	SIG OF F
LC	3.00000	11.00000	. . .	1.63636	.248
QC	.44444	5.00000	. . .	.53333	.493

FIG. 7.47. Table showing the simple interaction of the linear trend of A and the linear and quadratic trends of C (at the first level of factor B), in a three factor design with two repeated measures (B and C). The labels at the left of the rows will be misleading, and should be ignored. Although these RENAME labels will be useful for the main effect analyses, they will not be useful for the simple effects tests. The first row will give the linear, and the second the quadratic trends of factor C, in interaction with the linear trend of A. The table heading, by including A(1), indicates that the interaction is with the linear trend of A. Figure 7.20 offers a program that would produce this table. In Fig. 7.20 the request for trend analyses on the between subjects factor A does not appear until the third design subcommand, so this figure would appear under the major heading DESIGN 3, which would help to both locate it and identify it.

* * * * * * * * * * * ANALYSIS OF VARIANCE -- DESIGN 3 * * * *
TESTS INVOLVING 'C WITHIN B(1)' WITHIN-SUBJECT EFFECT.

AVERAGED TESTS OF SIGNIFICANCE FOR MEAS. 1 UNIQUE SUMS OF SQUARES

SOURCE OF VARIATION	SS	DF	MS	F	SIG OF F
WITHIN CELLS	16.00	12	1.33		
C WITHIN B(1)	83.19	2	41.59	31.19	.000
A(1) BY C WITHIN B(1)	3.44	2	1.72	1.29	.310
A(2) BY C WITHIN B(1)	2.48	2	1.24	.44	.657

FIG. 7.48. Table showing tests of the simple effects, for factor A, of its linear and quadratic trend interactions with factor C (at the first level of repeated measures factor B). This table is from a three factor design, with two repeated measures (B and C), shown in the program in Fig. 7.20. The WITHIN CELLS row offers the error term. The numerators in the F ratios, and the F tests, are found in the rows A(1) BY C WITHIN B(1), and A(2) BY C WITHIN B(1). The C WITHIN B(1) row offers a test of the simple effect of factor C, at the first level of factor B, which is also found in another table within the printout. Separate tables would present the tests for the different levels of factor B.

Whereas Fig. 7.42 offers a table for the interaction of a between subjects factor's trend with a repeated measures factor, Fig. 7.41 offers a table for the interaction of a repeated measures factor's trend with a between subjects factor.

Simple Trends

Figure 7.43 offers a table illustrating simple effects of the linear trend on a between subjects factor, A, in a two factor completely randomized design.

Figure 7.44 offers a table illustrating the simple effects of repeated measures trends as requested in Fig. 7.17.

```
* * * * * * * * * * ANALYSIS OF VARIANCE -- DESIGN 3 * * * *
TESTS INVOLVING 'MWITHIN C(1)' WITHIN-SUBJECT EFFECT.

TESTS OF SIGNIFICANCE FOR T1 UNIQUE SUMS OF SQUARES
```

SOURCE OF VARIATION	SS	DF	MS	F	SIG OF F
WITHIN CELLS	70.57	54	1.31		
MWITHIN C(1)	396.25	1	396.25	303.21	.000
A(1) BY MWITHIN C(1)	.21	1	4.96	3.80	.687
A(2) BY MWITHIN C(1)	4.96	1	4.96	3.80	.057
B(1) BY MWITHIN C(1)	.13	1	.13	.10	.756
B(2) BY MWITHIN C(1)	3.43	1	3.43	2.62	.111
A(1) BY B(1) BY MWIT HIN C(1)	1.71	1	1.71	1.31	.257
A(1) BY B(2) BY MWIT HIN C(1)	1.29	1	1.29	.98	.326

FIG. 7.49. Table giving several tests from a three factor design with two between subjects factors, A and B. This was produced by the program given in Figure 7.31. The one table includes the simple effects of the individual trends of A and contrasts of B, and as the last two tests, the simple interactions that were requested. The WITHIN CELLS row offers the error term for the F ratios in the table, while the row labeled MWITHIN C(1) is not relevant for this design.

```
EFFECT .. MWITHIN A(1) BY B BY C (CONT.)
UNIVARIATE F-TESTS WITH (1,6) D. F.
```

VARIABLE	HYPOTH. SS	ERROR SS	. . .	F	SIG OF F
LB	3.70370	4.55556	. . .	4.87805	.069
QB	16.00000	21.00000	. . .	4.57143	.076
C1	1.23457	7.62963	. . .	.97087	.363
C2	.59259	4.44444	. . .	.80000	.406

FIG. 7.50. Simple interactions between the trend on one repeated measures factor (B), and the contrasts on the other repeated measures factor (C), at the first level of a between subjects factor (A). This table was produced by the program in Fig. 7.34 of this chapter. The labels in the left hand column are from the RENAME subcommand, but are not useful for this table. The interactions have to be recognized by their order. The order of the labels for the interactions follow the usual order of the most slowly changing first interacting with the faster changing, only the latter changing, until all changes have taken place. The first row is the interaction of the linear trend of B with the first contrast of C, the second row is the interaction of the linear trend of B with the second contrast of C, the third is the interaction of the quadratic trend of B with the first contrast of C, and the last is the interaction of the quadratic trend of B with the second contrast of C.

The names in the RENAME subcommand used in the illustrative program in Fig. 7.17 would guide you through the printout for the main effect trends and their interactions. However, these RENAME labels would not be helpful for the tests of simple trends. You have to recognize the different trends by the order in which they appear in the table, the first row referring

EFFECT .. MWITHIN A(1) WITHIN B(1) BY C (CONT.)
UNIVARIATE F-TESTS WITH (1,54) D. F.

VARIABLE	HYPOTH. SS	ERROR SS	. . .	F	SIG OF F
LINEAR	.17857	45.35716	. . .	.21260	.647
QUADRA	34.32143	84.35714	. . .	21.97036	.000
CUBIC	4.46429	49.50000	. . .	4.87013	.032

FIG. 7.51. Simple simple effects of the trends on repeated measures factor C in a three factor mixed design, with one repeated measure, C. In this table the linear, quadratic and cubic trends on factor C are each tested within the first level of factor A at the first level of factor B. Separate tables give the tests at the different levels of factor B that were requested in the program (presented in this chapter in Fig. 7.24).

* * * * * * * * * * ANALYSIS OF VARIANCE -- DESIGN 3 * * * *
TESTS INVOLVING 'MWITHIN C(1)' WITHIN-SUBJECT EFFECT

TESTS OF SIGNIFICANCE FOR T1 USING UNIQUE SUMS OF SQUARES

SOURCE OF VARIATION	SS	DF	MS	F	SIG OF F
WITHIN CELLS	70.57	54	1.31		
MWITHIN C(1)	396.25	1	396.25	303.21	.000
B(1) WITHIN A(1) BY MWITHIN C(1)	2.38	1	2.38	1.82	.183
B(2) WITHIN A(1) BY MWITHIN C(1)	1.17	1	1.17	.89	.349

FIG. 7.52. Simple simple trends on between subjects factor B in a three factor mixed design, with one repeated measure, C. In this table, both the linear trend on factor B, labeled B(1), and the quadratic trend, labeled B(2), are tested within the first level of A and the first level of C, yielding F values of 1.82 and .89, respectively. The row labeled MWITHIN C(1) is not meaningful for this design. The presence of the word BY in the row labels indicate the rows offering the requested tests. Separate tables are used for the different levels of C at which the B contrasts are tested. Figure 7.25 in this chapter offers a program that would produce this table.

to the linear trend, the second row to the quadratic trend, etc. The table heading B WITHIN C(1) indicates that these are the trend tests concerning factor B, at the first level of factor C. Different tables would be used for each level of C.

Figure 7.45 offers a table for the simple effect trends on the between subjects factor, A, in a two factor mixed design.

Figure 7.46 offers a table for the simple trends on a repeated measures factor C in a two factor mixed design.

Figure 7.47 offers an example of a table that would give the tests for the interaction of the linear trend of A and the trends of C, at the first level of B, in a three factor design with two repeated measures (B and C).

Suppose that, instead of the simple effect of the interactions, one wished to obtain the simple effect of the interaction of the linear trend of A, with factor C, at the first level of factor B, and the same analysis for the quadratic trend of A. This is different than an interaction of trends, since only the

```
* * * * * * * * * * ANALYSIS OF VARIANCE -- DESIGN  3 * * * *
TESTS INVOLVING 'MWITHIN C(1) WITHIN B(1)' WITHIN-SUBJECT EFFECT.

TESTS OF SIGNIFICANCE FOR T1 USING UNIQUE SUMS OF SQUARES
SOURCE OF VARIATION         SS        DF        MS          F       SIG OF F

WITHIN CELLS              12.67        6       2.11
MWITHIN C(1) WITHIN       87.11        1      87.11        41.25      .001
B(1)
A(1) BY MWITHIN C(1)       8.17        1       8.17         3.87      .097
  WITHIN B(1)
```

FIG. 7.53. Simple simple trends on between subjects factor A in a three factor mixed design, with two repeated measures, B and C. In this table the linear trend on factor A, labeled A(1), is tested within the first level of B and the first level of C, yielding an F value of 3.87. The presence of the word BY in the row label indicates the row with the desired F test. The row labeled WITHIN CELLS presents the error term for the F ratio. The middle row is not relevant for this design. Separate tables are used for the different levels of B at which the trends of A are tested. If simple simple trends on both the linear and quadratic trends of A, A(1) and A(2), were requested, they would appear in the same table. Figure 7.26 of this chapter offers a program that would produce the table in this figure.

```
EFFECT .. MWITHIN A(1) BY C WITHIN B(1) (CONT.)
UNIVARIATE F-TESTS WITH (1,6) D. F.

VARIABLE      HYPOTH. SS      ERROR SS    . . .             F       SIG OF F

LC             48.16667        3.66667    . . .         78.81818      .000
QC              1.38889        4.33333    . . .          1.92308      .215
```

FIG. 7.54. Simple simple trends on repeated measures factor C in a three factor mixed design, with two repeated measures, B and C. In this table the linear and quadratic trends on factor C are each tested within the first level of factor A at the first level of factor B. Separate tables give the tests at the different levels of factor B that were requested in the program presented in this chapter in Fig. 7.27. The row labels, LC and QC, can vary, and so may not be informative in this case. They could turn out to be any of the labels used in the RENAME subcommand. The different trends for factor C have to be distinguished by their placement. The first (uppermost) row refers to the simple simple linear trend on C, and the second row to the simple simple quadratic trend on C, regardless of the row labels.

trends of A are involved in this interaction. Figure 7.48 offers the general form for the table giving these tests. Figure 7.20 provides a program that would produce such a table.

Figure 7.49 presents a table which includes the tests for the simple interaction of two between subject factors, trends on one and contrasts on the other, within a repeated measures factor C.

Figure 7.50 offers a table of simple interactions between the trend on one repeated measures factor (B), and the contrasts on the other repeated measures factor (C), at the first level of a between subjects factor (A).

Simple Simple Trends

Figure 7.51 offers a table indicating some simple simple effects of the trends of a repeated measures factor, C, in a three factor design with one repeated measure (C).

Figure 7.52 illustrates a table offering some simple simple trends of one of the between subjects factors, B, in a three factor design with one repeated measure C.

Figure 7.53 offers a table for some simple simple trends on the between subjects factor A in a three factor mixed design with two repeated measures, B and C.

Figure 7.54 offers a table for simple simple trends of the repeated measures factor C in a three factor mixed design with two repeated measures, B and C.

Index

(Commands, subcommands, and key words appear in upper case)